Advanced IGBO LANGUAGE

A Simplified Guide to Igbo Orthography
Phonology, Morphology and Lexicology

Elisha O. Ogbonna

Advanced Igbo Language by Elisha O. Ogbonna

This book is written to provide educational and Igbo language learning information for linguistic and advanced learners.

Copyright © March 2022 by Elisha O. Ogbonna

All rights reserved. No part of this book may be reproduced, transmitted, or distributed in any form by any means, including, but not limited to, recording, photocopying, or taking screenshots of parts of the book, without prior written permission from the author or the publisher. Brief quotations for noncommercial purposes, such as book reviews, permitted by Fair Use of the Canada Copyright Law, are allowed without written permissions, as long as such quotations do not cause damage to the book's commercial value. For permissions, write to the publisher, whose address is stated below.

ISBN:
978-1-7777461-3-1 (Hardcover)
978-1-7777461-2-4 (Paperback)
978-1-7777461-4-8 (eBook)

Manufactured in the Canada
Prinoelio Press
For Igbo Learning Hub
E-mail: Igbolearninghub@gmail.com
https://www.Igbo learninghub.com

Dedication

To my daughters,

Amanda and **Rebecca**
Without whom this book would have been completed months earlier.

ADVANCED IGBO LANGUAGE

Table of Contents

Dedication 3

Introduction 9

Guide to Pronunciation 11

Part One: 15

Igbo Orthography (Ederede Igbo) 15

Chapter 1 17

Introduction to Orthography (Okwu Mmalite Usoro Odide Asụsụ) 17

Chapter 2 25

Development of Igbo Orthography (Nkwalite Usoro Odide Asụsụ Igbo) 25

Chapter 3 51

Igbo Alphabet (Mkpụrụedemede Igbo) 51

Chapter 4 71

Spelling and spelling rules (Nsupe na Iwu Nsupe) 71

Chapter 5 79

Linguistic Ambiguity in Igbo Language (Mgbagwoju Anya di n'Asụsụ Igbo) 79

Chapter 6 89

Solutions to Igbo linguistic Ambiguity 89

(Idozi Mgbagwoju Anya di n'Asụsụ Igbo) 89

Chapter 7 99

Punctuation in Igbo Language (Akara Edemede di n'Asụsụ Igbo)99

Part Two: 105

Phonology & Phonetics (Ọdịdị ụdaasụsụ na Amụmàmụ Ụdaasụsụ) 105

Chapter 8 107

Phonetics & Phonology in Igbo language: 107

Chapter 9 111

Principles of Phonemic Analysis (Usoro Ịkọwa mkpụrụụdasụsụ). 111

Chapter 10 117

Classification of Phoneme (Nkèụdị Mkpụrụụdaasụsụ) 117

Chapter 11 129

The organ of speech (Njiakpọ Okwu) 129

Chapter 12 137

Place of Articulation (Ebe Mkpọpụta Ụda) 137

Chapter 13 151

Transcription of Igbo Phonemes (Ndepụtagharị Mkpụrụụdaasụsụ Igbo) 151

Chapter 14 155

Articulatory Phonetics (Amụmàmụ Mkpọpụta Ụdaasụsụ) 155

Part Three: 165

Morphology of Igbo Linguistic (Amụmàmụ Mkpụruasụsụ nke Mmụta Asụsụ Igbo) 165

Chapter 15 167

The nature of Igbo Morpheme (Amụmàmụ Ọdịdị nke Mkpụruasụsụ Igbo) 167

Chapter 16 175

The Classification of Igbo Morpheme (Nkewasị Mkpụrụasụsụ Igbo) 175

Chapter 17 179

Morphological Process of Igbo Word 179

Chapter 18 197

Allomorphs in Igbo Language 197

(Ndịiche Mkpụrụasụsụ nke Igbo) 197

Part Four: 209

Lexicology in Igbo Linguistics (Amụmàmụ Ụdịdị, Nghọta na Itinye Mkpụrụokwu Igbo N'ọrụ) 209

Chapter 19 211

Introduction to Lexicology 211

(Mmalite Amụmàmụ Nghọta Mkpụrụokwu) 211

Chapter 20 221

Word Building (Word Formation) 221

(Usoro Mmụba Okwu Igbo) 221

Chapter 21 245

Synonyms and Antonyms 245

(Myiri Mkpụrụokwu na Okwu Mmegide) 245

Chapter 22 277

Parts of Speech 277

(Nkejiasụsụ Igbo) 277

Index 293

ADVANCED IGBO LANGUAGE

Introduction

For many years, I was asked by someone who learned that I taught Igbo language in school to start an online class in order to teach people who would be interested to learn the language. But I brushed it off because I was too busy with work and other self-help book I was writing at that time. I did not consider it as something too necessary because of the dwindling and disappearing usage of the language due the popular embrace and preference of learning to speak and write in English by many Igbo speakers.

Then, the Covid-19 pandemic hit and I was forced to stay at home as much as everyone else when lockdown was authorized. That long time of unemployment got me into looking at Igbo language as Igbo language YouTube channels were on the increase and many people were showing interest on getting to know their ancestry and the language. It hit me. I wanted to use that time to start something.

I decided to start with writing Igbo language books. This was the best option for me since many of my zoom meetings and online programs that I was having at the time were frequently interrupted by my kids who were as well forced to stay home by the pandemic. I then, picked up my pen and started writing. That led to the publishing of my first book, "Comprehensive Igbo Language;" which was for beginners and intermediate learners.

Two years later, I thought to myself that I need to move up higher to produce a resource for people who already have the skill of speaking and writing the language and train teachers of the language. An advanced book came to my mind. I, without much hesitation, decided to put forward another book that would serve as a textbook to learners in both high and tertiary institutions worldwide.

Today, you have in your hand, a clear, detailed and most-up-to-date Igbo language book that gives a straightforward description and greater knowledge on Igbo language orthography, spelling rules, solution to linguistic ambiguities, word formation, class changing and maintaining, organ of speech, place of articulation and many more.

Guide to Pronunciation

Igbo language pronunciation is a reflection of spelling and tonal markings. The pronunciation of each letter is subject to have precise and consistent rules of identifying the sound associated with that particular letter. Words are pronounced by adding together the sounds of each individual letter.

Vowels

Letter	Pronounced like	Examples
a	the *a* in apple and again	aka, akpa, Amerika
e	the *e* in essay and eternal	ekwe, eke, egbe
I	the i in elise and *e* in easy	igbe, ikpere, imi
ị	the *i* in iguana and *i* in inch	ịgba, ịchafụ, ịsha
o	the *o* in orange and owner	okwe, oke, okwu
ọ	the *or* in organ and corn	ọka, ọkwa, ọma
u	the *u* in rule and *oo* in tool	ukwe, ukwu, ugo
ụ	the *u* in furrow and church	ụkwa, ụka, ụgba

Diagraphs

Letter	Pronounced like	Examples
ch	the *ch* in ouch and chum	ọcha, chukwu, ichie
gb	the *gb* is a linguistic letter	gbanye, ịgba, agbo
gh	the *gh* is a linguistic letter	aghara, agha, ghọta
gw	the *gui* in linguine	gwongworo, egwu
kp	the *kp* is a linguistic letter	ekpere, ikpere, Akpa
kw	the *que* in queenie	ekwe, akwa, okwa
nw	the *w* in winter	enwe, anwụ, onwụ
ny	the *ny* in new (BrE)	anya, anyanwu, enyi

sh   the *sh* in shampoo   isha, ọsha, ashiri

The pronunciation of diagraphs like gb, gh, and kp, whose English phonetic equivalent I could not provide, may be learned by listening to the sound of their pronunciations from my audiobook. You may also ask a proficient Igbo language speaker to help you with them.

Other consonants sound

Letter	Pronounced like	Examples
b	the *b* in bitter	ọbịa, ọbara, bọọlụ
d	the *d* in dig	ụdara, ọdachi, dabanye
f	the *f* in fish and fire	fọdụrụ, fopu, fecha
g	the *g* in give and gate	gaa, ụgụrụ, gawa
h	the *h* in heat and height	ọha, hapụ, ohụrụ
j	the *j* in jam and jean	jụrụ, jaachi, juputara
k	the *k* in kernel and keep	kedụ, onyeka, kasara
l	the *l* in latch and lean	laawa, lee, leta
m	the *m* in milk and mean	maka, mụrụ, ọmụmụ
n	the *n* in never and now	nọrọ, ọnọdụ, nnụnnụ
ṅ	the *ng* in strong and song	aṅụrị, aṅụ, ọṅu
p	the *p* in pillar and party	pụrụ, pụta, oporo
r	the *r* in reach and rain	racha, rụrụ, rịe, họrọ
s	the *s* in salt, self and sight	soro, sịrị, jịsịke
t	the *t* in tea and attach	taa, teta, tinye
v	the *v* in invite and vent	mvọ (isi), nwanvo
w	the *wea* in weather	kụwaa, were, wụrụ
y	the *y* in year and yield	yịri, ya, yọro,
z	the *z* in zebra and zion	zara, zụru, zoro

Tonal Marking (Akara Ụdaolu)

Tonal marking, also referred to as diacritical marks, are extra symbols that are placed above or below a letter to modify the pronunciation or to clarify the meaning of a word.

Igbo language is a tonal language with three distinctive tones: the high, mid and low. The following are the list of Igbo alphabets with their tonal accent marks, both in capital and small letters.

Examples:
Letter	Acute (High tone)	Macron (Mid tone)	Grave (Low tone)
a	Á á	Ā ā	À à

Examples:
ákwá - cry [high tone – high tone]
àkwá - egg [low tone – high tone]

Here are five tips that should help you perfect your pronunciation of words in Igbo language:

1. Begin with learning the alphabet's sounds.
2. Practice as many times as you can.
3. Try pronouncing three-letter words starting from breaking the Igbo word down into sounds: Example, [a] + [k] + [a] = aka and so on.
4. Say it out loud and exaggerate the sounds until you can consistently produce them.
5. If possible, record yourself saying the word in full sentences, then watch yourself and listen.

According to Greg Thomson, *"The only way to begin speaking a new language is to begin speaking badly."*

Part One:

Igbo Orthography (Ederede Igbo)

ADVANCED IGBO LANGUAGE

Chapter 1

Introduction to Orthography (Okwu Mmalite Usoro Odide Asụsụ)

Research has shown that there are at least 6,000 spoken languages in the world today. These spoken languages are expressed by a variety of writing systems to help in conveying written messages. The term that denotes this writing system is called "orthographies." The term "orthographic" comes from Greek, which means to have correct writing. Over 400 orthographies exist today.

Orthographies are the symbols used to represent spoken language. It is a system of visually representing a language in a written form. Thus, a written language that uses symbols for entire words is called a logographic orthography. Orthographies differ in the size of the sound unit that is represented by each symbol. Each of these orthographies can be classified as alphabetic or non-alphabetic.

Alphabetic orthographies
In alphabetic orthographies, each symbol represents an individual sound called a phoneme (e.g., the/b/sound in "book" is one

phoneme). There are several different alphabets that are used to create written languages. For example, English uses the Latin alphabet, and 26 symbols (letters), to represent the spoken language. Norwegian and Slovak also use the Latin alphabet, with extra three vowels not used in English (å, æ, ø). Slovak uses an added series of accent marks to indicate how a letter is spoken (for example, ó or š), resulting into 46 symbols to represent the Slovak spoken language.

Igbo language, our subject of study, uses the Latin alphabet with an additional diacritical mark that alters the pronunciation of duplicated symbols or letters, resulting into 36 symbols to represent the Igbo spoken language. It uses three accent marks to indicate tone not sound. This makes it 10 symbols less than Slovak. Slovak 46 symbols (letters) make it the longest Slavic and European alphabet. Most European languages, including Czech, Danish, Dutch, English, Finnish, French, German, Hungarian, Icelandic, Italian, Norwegian, Polish, Portuguese, Slovak, Spanish, Swedish, Turkish, and Welsh use the Latin alphabet.

Other alphabetic orthographies include Cyrillic, Devanagari, Greek, Hangul alphabet, etc. and a combination of Latin and Cyrillic. Cyrillic alphabet is the type of alphabet that uses different sets of symbols to represent the spoken language, but at the level of the phoneme, it still codes the spoken language. The Cyrillic alphabet is used for Bulgarian, Russian, and Ukrainian spoken languages. The Devanagari alphabet is used for Hindi, one of the official languages of India. The Greek alphabet is only used for the Greek language. The Hangul alphabeti is used for the Korean language. Some languages, such as the South Slavic language spoken in Serbia, Croatia (Serbo-Croat), use the combination of

Latin and the Cyrillic alphabets. Hebrew and Arabic are sometimes classified as abjads. It is a symbol used to represent a spoken language that only contains consonants, and not vowels. It is called an "abjad", because generally vowels are not included when writing them. However, a lot has changed from the past in the representation of "abjad." Nowadays, the use of accent marks to show where a vowel should be has led to many people to classify both Hebrew and Arabic written symbols as alphabets, not abjads.

In alphabetic languages, the smallest meaningful contrastive unit in a writing system (graphemes) represents phonemes or individual sounds. This is evident in alphabetic language, like English, other European languages such as French, German, Italian, Spanish, as well as in Arabic, Hebrew, and Korean Hangul. On the contrary, Japanese kana or Cherokee use a syllabic writing system in which each grapheme represents a syllable. Whereas, Chinese, Japanese Kanji, and Korean Hanja use a morphographic writing system in which each grapheme represents a morpheme or a unit of meaning.

In alphabetic orthographies, when each letter is pronounced the same way, the mapping is said to be "consistent" and the orthography is called "shallow." There is always a match up in how the phonemes (sounds) and the graphemes (symbols or letters) are presented. In German, Igbo, Italian, Spanish, almost every letter represents only one sound which makes their mapping consistent. On the other hand, when each letter is pronounced in more than one way, the mapping is said to be "inconsistent" and the orthography is called "deep." There is no match up in how the phonemes (sounds) and the graphemes (symbols or letters) are presented. A letter can have many pronunciations, such as the two different/a/sounds in "apple" and "aid." In English and Danish, many letters represent more than one sound which makes their mapping inconsistent. As a result, researchers for the most part agree that Finnish, German, Greek, Italian, Korean, Serbo-Croat, Spanish, and Turkish are relatively shallow or consistent orthographies, while Danish, French, Portuguese, etc. contain more inconsistent mappings in phonemes and graphemes match up. English is the most inconsistent language in the world because it has 26 letters against 44 graphemes. That is 18 more additional smallest meaningful contrastive units in a writing system.

Non-alphabetic orthographies

Non-alphabetic orthographies represent either the syllable or a one-syllable unit of meaning with each symbol. A unit of spoken language is represented by a symbol, in a similar fashion as the alphabetic orthographies, but unlike alphabetic orthographies, that unit of spoken language is larger than just a phoneme. For example, people often referred to Chinese as a pictograph (a language made up of pictures), because the characters are pictures of the words they represent. In reality, very few Chinese characters are actually pictures of the words they represent.

Cherokee, Tamil, or Japanese Kana orthographies represent their syllable while Chinese, Japanese Kanji symbol represent a unit of pronunciation (a syllable) that is also a unit of meaning. Chinese orthography and writing system is considered a morpho-syllabic system. This is because about 80–90% of Chinese characters contain what is called a phonetic radical. A phonetic radical is just one part of the character that provides a clue as to how to say the word.

In summary, all orthographies represent spoken language with written symbols. Some orthographies have some similarities among themselves (e.g. alphabetic orthographies).

Layers of Igbo orthography
Igbo orthography is the system of writing conventions used to represent spoken Igbo in written form, allowing readers to connect the graphemes to sound and to meaning. It includes Igbo's norms of spelling, hyphenation, capitalization, word breaks, emphasis, and punctuation. There are three layers of Igbo orthography or spelling, namely the alphabet layer, the pattern layer and the meaning layer.

Alphabet layer: represents one-on-one correspondence between letter and sound. In this layer, students use the sound of individual letter to accurately spell words. In Igbo alphabetic orthographies, each letter is pronounced exactly the same way in all expression, the mapping is consistent. Since there is always a match up in how the phonemes (sounds) and the graphemes (symbols or letters) are presented, students would have to grapple with the number of sounds to learn and nothing more.

Pattern layer: As there are 44 sounds in English but only 26 letters in the alphabet, English learners would have to explore the combinations of sound spellings that form visual and auditory patterns associated with the 44 phonemes. In this layer, unlike English learners, Igbo students would have to learn the pattern of vowels combinations and the permissibility that is granted to word combination as well as loan words. All these will be discussed in details in other following chapters.

Meaning layer: meaning layer is when Igbo students learn that groups of letters can represent meaning directly. This includes the derivations associated with prefixes, suffixes, and verb root in the formation of words from units or groups of morphemes. Morphemes are the smallest units of meaning in language.

Three Phases of Learning to Read

Orthographic reading skills refer to the ability to identify patterns of specific letters as words, eventually leading to word recognition. With development of these skills, reading becomes an automatic process. When learning to read, one of the most fundamental processes for learners is the understanding of the relationships between printed text and spoken language. Orthography refers to the language-specific variations in these relationships.

The first phase can be considered a *pictorial stage*, when the learner's brain photographs words and visually adjusts to the shape of the alphabet's letters. The visual symbols that represent individual sounds in a spoken language known as phonemes are gradually identified and learned.

The second phase is the *phonological stage*, when the brain begins to decode the letters (graphemes) into sounds (phonemes). The visual symbols that represent individual sounds in a spoken language known as phonemes are gradually committed to memory. The students become more confident with letters arrangements.

The third phase is the *orthographic stage*, when the language learner is able to recognize words quickly and accurately. More confidence in spelling and pronunciation are the indicators of this phase. Reading material in the language become less worrisome as students continuously learn new words and build their vocabulary.

Orthographic Mapping
Linnea Ehri coined the term "orthographic mapping". Orthographic Mapping is the process through which a reader can fully analyze sounds in spoken words and match those sounds to printed words. Kilpatrick (2015) describes orthographic mapping as 'the mental process we use to permanently store words for immediate, effortless retrieval.'

Orthographic mapping has been known about since the late 1970s, and was first described by Linnea Ehri, when her work in the 1980s provided evidence for her Orthographic Mapping Theory. Spelling becomes mapped onto pronunciations and these "mapping connections" serve as the glue to hold these words in memory.

It is the process we use to take an unfamiliar printed word and turn it into an immediately recognizable word'. Orthographic mapping (OM) involves the formation of letter-sound connections to bond the spellings, pronunciations, and meanings of specific words in memory. It explains how language learners learn to read words by sight, to spell words from memory, and to acquire vocabulary words from print.

Chapter 2

Development of Igbo Orthography (Nkwalite Usoro Odide Asụsụ Igbo)

Orthography is a set of conventions for writing a language. Igbo language has had two types of orthographies from inception until now. These orthographies could be classified as ancient orthography and modern orthography. The two types of Igbo orthography are: Nsibidi and Abịịdịị. This chapter will look into the history of both orthographies and why modern orthography is preferable, predominant and premminent.

Nsibidi System of Writing
Nsibidi (also known as nsibiri, nchibiddi or nchibiddy) is a system of symbols or proto-writing developed in the former eastern part of Nigeria prior to colonization. Proto-writing consists of visible marks communicating limited information. Nsibidi systems emerged from earlier traditions of symbol systems in the early Neolithic, as early as the 7th millennium BC. The Neolithic period is the final division of the Stone

Age. The Stone Age was a broad prehistoric period during which stone was widely used to make tools with an edge, a point, or a percussion surface. The period lasted for roughly 3.4 million years and ended between 4,000 BCE and 2,000 BCE, with the advent of metalworking.

Nsibidi used ideographic or early mnemonic symbols or both to represent a limited number of concepts, in contrast to true writing systems, which record the language of the writer. Ideographic is a graphic symbol that represents an idea or concept, independent of any particular language, and specific words or phrases. Some ideograms are comprehensible only by familiarity with prior convention; others convey their meaning through pictorial resemblance to a physical object, and thus may also be referred to as pictograms.

Mnemonic is any learning technique that aids information retention or retrieval (remembering) in the human memory for better understanding. Mnemonics make use of elaborative encoding, retrieval cues, and imagery as specific tools to encode information in a way that allows for efficient storage and retrieval. Mnemonics aid original information in becoming associated with something more accessible or meaningful—which, in turn, provides better retention of the information.

Nsibidi are classified as pictograms, though there have been suggestions that some are logograms or syllabograms. A logogram or logograph is a written character that represents a word or morpheme. Syllabograms, on the other hand, are signs used to write the syllables (or morae) of words. This term is most often used in the context of a writing system otherwise organized on different principles, three of which—alphabet symbols mostly represent phonemes, logographic script symbols represent morphemes—but a system based mostly on syllabograms is a syllabary (they represent the syllables or moras which make up words).

The use of the Nsibidi symbol system was first described in 1904.[1] Excavation of terracotta vessels, headrests, and anthropomorphic figurines from the Calabar region of southeast Nigeria, dated to roughly the 5th to 15th centuries, revealed "an iconography readily comparable" to nsibidi.[2] The origin of nsibidi is attributed to the Ejagham people in Northern Cross River. Nsibidi spread throughout the region and was adopted by other cultures and art such as the Igbo uri or uli graphic design.[3] In 1909 J. K. Macgregor who collected Nsibidi symbols claimed that nsibidi was formed by the Uguakima, Ebe or Uyanga subgroups of the Igbo people, which legend says were taught the script by baboons.[4]

However, the Nsibidi of the Ejagham people predates these events and it is believed that Macgregor had been misled by his informants.[5] There are several hundred nsibidi symbols. They were

---

[1] Gregersen, Edgar A. *(1977). Language in Africa: An Introductory Survey.* CRC Press. p. 176. ISBN 0-677-04380-5.
[2] Slogar, Christopher *(2005). Eyo, Ekpo (ed.). Iconography and Continuity in West Africa: Calabar Terracottas and the Arts of the Cross River Region of Nigeria/Cameroon.* University of Maryland. pp. 58–62.
[3] Slogar, Christopher *(Spring 2007). "Early Ceramics from Calabar, Nigeria: Towards a History of Nsibidi".* African Arts. University of California. 40 (1): 18–29. doi:10.1162/afar.2007.40.1.18. S2CID 57566625.
[4] Diringer, David *(1953). The Alphabet: A Key to the History of Mankind.* Philosophical Library. pp. 148–149.
[5] West African journal of archaeology". *West African Archaeological Association.* WAJA by Oxford University Press. 21: 105. 1991.

once taught in a school to children.[6] Many of the signs deal with love affairs; those that deal with warfare and the sacred are kept secret.[7] Nsibidi is used on wall designs, calabashes, metals (such as bronze), leaves, swords, and tattoos.[8] It is primarily used by the Ekpe Leopard Society (also known as Ngbe or Egbo), a secret society that is found across Cross River State among the Ekoi, Efik, Igbo people, Bahumono and other nearby peoples.

Before the colonial era of Nigeria history, nsibidi was divided into a sacred version and a public, more decorative version which could be used by women.[9] Aspects of colonial rule such as Western education and Christian doctrine drastically reduced the number of nsibidi-literate people, leaving the secret society members as some of the last literate in the symbols.[10] Nsibidi was and is still a means of transmitting Ekpe symbolism. Nsibidi was transported to Cuba and Haiti via the Atlantic slave trade, where it developed into the anaforuana and veve symbols.

Abịdịị System of Writing

---

[6] Isichei, Elizabeth Allo *(1997)*. *A History of African Societies to 1870*. Nsibidi: Cambridge University Press. p. *357*. *ISBN* *0-521-45599-5*
[7] [sichei, Elizabeth Allo *(1997)*. *A History of African Societies to 1870*. Nsibidi: Cambridge University Press. p. *357*. *ISBN* *0-521-45599-5*
[8] Elechi, O. Oko *(2006)*. Doing Justice without the State: The Afikpo (Ehugbo) Nigeria Model. CRC Press. p. 98. ISBN 0-415-97729-0.]; [Rothenberg, Jerome; Rothenberg, Diane *(1983)*. *Symposium of the Whole: A Range of Discourse Toward an Ethnopoetics*. University of California Press. pp. *285–286*. *ISBN* *0-520-04531-9*.
[9] Rothenberg, Jerome; Rothenberg, Diane *(1983)*. *Symposium of the Whole: A Range of Discourse Toward an Ethnopoetics*. University of California Press. pp. *285–286*. *ISBN* *0-520-04531-9*.
[10] Slogar, Christopher *(2005)*. Eyo, Ekpo (ed.). *Iconography and Continuity in West Africa: Calabar Terracottas and the Arts of the Cross River Region of Nigeria/Cameroon* (PDF). University of Maryland. p. 155.

Prior to Abịdịị system of writing, a form of writing called *nsibidi*, existed among the Igbo and neighboring groups before 15th centuries. It eventually fizzled out, probably because of evolution of alphabet system or its popular use among secret societies whose members limited its teachings and exposure to the younger generation who will end up not knowing that it was once a public system of communication and writing.

In 1904, T. D. Maxwell, Acting District Commissioner in Calabar, was the first European to learn about the existence of *nsibidi*. Apart from *nsibidi* writing, the Igbo acculturated themselves effectively by informal methods.[11]

There are five developmental periods of Igbo alphabetic system of writing, namely: the Isuawa Igbo studies, the union Igbo studies, the great orthography controversy period, the SPILC development period and the standard Igbo period. Each of these periods came after the extinction of Nsibidi and the inhuman slave trade that forced many Africans to migrate to North America and West Indies between 15th to q7th centuries.

The Isuama Igbo Studies period (1766-1900)
Between 1766-1900, Isuama Igbo studies period was the answer to the disappearing Nsibidi system. It was used as a type of dialect that represented a common standard dialect by emancipated slaves of Igbo origin that settled in Sierra Leone and Fernando Po (now part of Equatorial Guinea) in the 1800s. Around 1766, G. C. A.

---

[11] *Louis Nnamdi Oraka,* **The Foundations of Igbo Studies** *(Onitsha: University Publishing Company, 1983 pp. 13, 17.*

Oldendorp, a German missionary of the Moravian Brethren, went to their West Indies Caribbean mission.[12]

And by 1777, Oldendorp produced a book, **Geschichte der Mission der Evangelischen Bruder auf den Carabischen** (History of the Evangelistic Mission of the Brothers in the Caribbean). The book contained few Igbo words, numerals, 13 nouns, 2 sentences. As a result, he was the first person to publish a material that contains Igbo words and expression. As time progresses, in 1789, **The Life of Olaudah Equiano, or Gustavus Vassa The African** (London, 1789), written by a former slave, mentioned 79 Igbo words.[13] A good modern edition: London: Dawsons of Pall Mall, 1969 (2 vols; ed. by Paul Edwards).

By late 1700 and early 1800, Igbo language study transferred from the West Indies and London to Freetown, Sierra Leone, and Fernando Po, because freed slaves were settled there, the larger number in Freetown.[14]

In 1828, Mrs. Hannah Kilham, a Quaker mission teacher, published *Specimens of African Languages Spoken in the Colony of Sierra-Leone*. A material that included: Igbo numerals and some 50 Igbo nouns. Three years later, Mrs. Kilham started a girls' school at Charlotte village, Sierra Leone. Formal education in

---

[12] Louis Nnamdi Oraka, *The Foundations of Igbo Studies (Onitsha: University Publishing Company, 1983 p. 20.*
[13] Louis Nnamdi Oraka, *The Foundations of Igbo Studies (Onitsha: University Publishing Company, 1983 p. 21.*
[14] Louis Nnamdi Oraka, *The Foundations of Igbo Studies (Onitsha: University Publishing Company, 1983 p. 65.*

vernacular languages is begun. In 1837, MacGregor Laird published the wordlist he collected inside the Igbo homeland during his two-year Niger Expedition of 1832-1834. Six years later, in 1840, Jacob Friedrich Schon, German missionary, reported that he had collected 1600 words in the Igbo language. His report remained unpublished. A year later, in 1841, Edwin Norris, Assistant Secretary, Royal Asiatic Society, compiled wordlists from West and Central African languages to use in Niger expeditions. He used Laird's 70 words and others from two unknown sources (a manuscript, and an Igbo living in London).[15]

The same year, in another Norris expedition on the Niger, he took two missionary linguists from the staff of the CMS (Church Missionary Society) in Freetown, J. F. Schon and Samuel Ajayi Crowther (the latter a Yoruba-born ex-slave and teacher), along with twelve interpreters, including Igbo who came from emancipated slave families that settled in Freetown. John Christopher Taylor and Simon Jonas were among them. No permanent mission was founded. Schon was interested in Igbo and Hausa. At a stopover in Aboh, he tried to communicate in Igbo but was disappointed that people did not understand him. He then abandoned Igbo study for some twenty years.[16]

These missionaries continue in their quest to develop a common system of written communication. Between 1843 and 1848 Morrick (missionary in Fernando Po) and John Clarke, Baptist

---

[15] Louis Nnamdi Oraka, *The Foundations of Igbo Studies* (Onitsha: University Publishing Company, 1983 p. 22

[16] *Louis Nnamdi Oraka, **The Foundations of Igbo Studies** (Onitsha: University Publishing Company, 1983 p. 23.*

missionary, together collected vocabularies of African languages. Clarke published them in 1848, including 250 words and a few numerals written in Igbo. 24 Igbo dialects were represented, including Aro, Bonny, Ndoli and Agbaja. In 1854, Lepsius, German philologist, produced international "Standard Alphabet" for all world languages to use.[17]

Additional fifty words were added in 1854 by S. W. Koelle, a German missionary, who published Polyglotta Africana, with a vocabulary gathered from liberated slaves in Sierra Leone. His publication contained some 300 Igbo words representing five dialects: Isoama, Isiele, Agbaja, Aro, Mbofia (Oraka p. 23). Two years later, in 1856, Crowther and Jonas stayed together in Lagos, where Jonas taught his master Igbo. A year later, in 1857, Crowther produced his first book in Igbo, with Jonas's help. **Isoama-Ibo Primer** has 17 pages, with the Igbo alphabet, words, phrases, sentence patterns, the Lord's Prayer, the Ten Commandments, and translations of the first chapters of Matthew's Gospel. Thus Crowther became the first to use the Lepsius "Standard Alphabet".[18]

It went fast after the publication of Lepsius "Standard Alphabet." In 1857, Dr. William Baikie's ship berthed at Onitsha. On board were Crowther and his missionary team, including Igbo speakers Simon Jonas and Rev. J. C. Taylor. Crowther established a mission and left it in Taylor's hands. In less than a week Taylor had opened

---

[17] *Louis Nnamdi Oraka*, **The Foundations of Igbo Studies** *(Onitsha: University Publishing Company, 1983 pp. 24, 25.*

[18] Louis Nnamdi Oraka, **The Foundations of Igbo Studies** *(Onitsha: University Publishing Company, 1983 pp. 23, 24, 25.*

a school for young girls. **Isoama-Ibo** Primer served as their textbook. In 1861, J. F. Schon picked up the tab and apparently resumed Igbo studies, publishing his **Oku Ibo: Grammatical Elements of the Ibo Language**, written in the Isuama dialect, using Lepsius orthography. In 1870, Church Missionary Society (CMS) in London used Lepsius orthography to publish **An Ibo Primer**, by F. W. Smart, a catechist posted in 1868 to the first outpost Christian Station in Niger Delta. Crowther, first Bishop of the Niger, posted him there with W. E. L. Carew. In the 1870s Smart and Carew each published an Igbo Primer and carried out translation works on church liturgy.[19]

In 1880, Crowther thought his Niger Mission was collapsing, since the Igbo dialect he chose was not a "living" dialect spoken by a particular group of the Igbo. The Church Missionary Society (CMS) realized its mistakes and decided to give up its effort to use one dialect only. In 1882 Crowther wrote **Vocabulary of the Ibo Language**, the first comprehensive dictionary in Igbo. In 1883 Crowther and Schon jointly revised it and added more words. They finally came out with **Vocabulary of the Ibo Language, Part II**, an English-Ibo dictionary. By this time, Igbo had had some 50 books and booklets published in it.[20]

In 1882, Britain enacted the first education ordinance to control and direct educational activities of Christian missions in what later became her West African colonies. It provided grants-in-aid conditional on the teaching of reading and writing of the English

---

[19] Louis Nnamdi Oraka, *The Foundations of Igbo Studies (Onitsha: University Publishing Company, 1983 pp. 25, 26.*
[20] Louis Nnamdi Oraka, *The Foundations of Igbo Studies (Onitsha: University Publishing Company, 1983 p. 27.*

language only. This caused a stalemate in the development of many West African languages. As a result, in 1885, Roman Catholic Mission (RCM) reached Igboland but did not seem to be interested in the study of the Igbo language.[21]

Sadly, in 1891, Bishop Crowther died (at over 80 years of age), and the Isuama-Igbo period died with him. By this time two young men, the Englishman T. J. Dennis and the Sierra Leonean Henry Johnson, had joined the mission. In 1892, Julius Spencer, an Onitsha-based Sierra Leonean missionary, published **An Elementary Grammar of the Igbo Language**. This was revised by Archdeacon Dennis in 1916.[22]

The Union Igbo Studies (1900-1929)
Between 1900 – 1929, Igbo orthography development entered into the Union Igbo Studies period. This period is commonly referred to as Igbo version developed by Church Missionary Society (CMS). It aimed at inclusiveness in binding or writing all Igbo dialects. As a result it used terms understood in Onitsha, Owerri, Unwana, Arochukwu and Bonny dialects, in its orthography keeping idioms and proverbs common to all. This version was intended to be a sort of "central" or "compromise" Igbo, playing the role of a literary medium for the Igbo people.

The most prominent work published in Union Igbo was the Holy Bible (Bible Nso). The Union Igbo period saw major translation works. Missionaries collected materials on Igbo culture, including

---

[21] Louis Nnamdi Oraka, *The Foundations of Igbo Studies* (Onitsha: University Publishing Company, 1983 pp. 28, 29.
[22] Louis Nnamdi Oraka, *The Foundations of Igbo Studies* (Onitsha: University Publishing Company, 1983 pp. 27, 30.

proverbs, folktales, riddles and customs.[23] Within this period (1900-1929), Rev. Thomas J. Dennis was the best, most prolific student of Igbo and writer of his time. He used an Igbo Language Translation Committee, including Igbo indigenes, to translate **Pilgrim's Progress** and some catechisms into Igbo. He also translated the **Union Reader** and the **Union Hymnal**. In 1917, he died in a shipwreck.[24]

A. Gabot, French missionary, produced a trilingual dictionary, **English-Ibo and French Dictionary** in 1904. A year later, in 1905, Niger Mission saw a need to adopt a compromise dialect if the Bible were to be translated into a generally understood Igbo. Church Missionary Society (CMS) sent Dennis from Onitsha to Owerri to see about locating the headquarters of Igbo language studies there. He went with Alphonsus Onyeabo, an Onitsha-born catechist who later became a bishop. Dennis reported that Egbu, near Owerri, would be the ideal site, because the purest Igbo dialect was spoken there. Church Missionary Society (CMS) approved it and Dennis, Onyeabo, and T. D. Anyaegbunam went to Egbu and opened a station. In 1907, P. C. Zappa, a French missionary, compiled a bilingual dictionary, **Essai de Dictionnaire Francais-Ibo ou Francais-Ika**, with the help of a catechist, Mr. Nwokeabia. Zappa rightly saw Ika as an Igbo dialect and not as a language in itself. And in 1909, Dennis and the others completed translation of the New Testament, the last part of their work. Lepsius orthography was used. Dennis replaced "ds,"

---

[23] Louis Nnamdi Oraka, *The Foundations of Igbo Studies* (Onitsha: University Publishing Company, 1983 pp. 28, 29.
[24] Louis Nnamdi Oraka, *The Foundations of Igbo Studies* (Onitsha: University Publishing Company, 1983 p. 28.

"ts" and "s" with "j," "ch" and "sh." Controversy ensued about the dialect used.[25]

In 1912, Rev. G. T. Basden published Niger Ibos, a collection of Igbo customs and traditions. Between 1913 - 1914, Northcote W. Thomas produced **Anthrological Report on the Igbo-Speaking People of Nigeria**, in 6 volumes. Part II and Part V were devoted to Igbo-English (based on Onitsha and Awka dialects) and English-Igbo (with many words from the western Igbo dialect of Asaba) dictionaries, respectively. In 1916, Archdeacon Dennis revised and enlarged Spencer's 1892 grammar. Four years later, in 1920 Phelps-Stokes Fund (American philanthropic organization interested in education of world's black people) sponsored two commissions to Africa. Subsequently (1922) it published **Report on Education in Africa: Study of West, South and Equatorial Africa**, recognizing the importance of the mother tongue in education of children. In 1923 Isaac Iwekanuno wrote the first historical essay in the Igbo language, **Akuko Ala Obosi**, in Obosi dialect. In 1925, The Phelps-Stokes Report prompted the British Colonial Office to set up an Advisory Committee on Native Education in its African colonies, stressing the importance of the vernaculars.[26]

In 1926, The Education Ordinance and Code was enacted, requiring that only the vernacular or English be media of instruction. The Board of Education in Nigeria was reorganized to conform to the provisions of the Ordinance. On June 29, 1926,

---

[25] Louis Nnamdi Oraka, *The Foundations of Igbo Studies (Onitsha: University Publishing Company, 1983 pp. 29 30.*
[26] Louis Nnamdi Oraka, *The Foundations of Igbo Studies (Onitsha: University Publishing Company, 1983 pp. 30, 31.*

linguists and others from Africa and Europe met in London and launched the International Institute of African Languages and Cultures (IIALC). In 1927, the International Institute of African Languages and Cultures (IIALC) published a pamphlet, **Practical Orthography of African Languages**. 8 vowels and 28 consonants, with "gw," "kw," and "nw" added for Igbo sounds. The pamphlet used some international phonetic symbols. This was a radical change from the Lepsius orthography used by Church Missionary Society (CMS) for nearly seventy years. It started a heated controversy that almost suspended Igbo studies for more than thirty years.[27]

The Great Orthography Controversy Period (1929-1961)

In 1929, the International Institute of African Languages and Culture (IIALC) member Prof. Westermann was invited to Nigeria to advise the Colonial Government on orthography for languages, including Igbo. He recommended the 1927 "Africa" orthography of the IIALC. The Board of Education agreed, and made efforts to replace the Lepsius orthography. The IIALC orthography became known as the "Adams-Ward" orthography because of two people in Eastern Nigeria who fought hard for its adoption: Mr. R. F. G. Adams, an Inspector of Education, and Dr. Ida C. Ward, a research linguist of the London School of Oriental and African Studies. Also, the Protestant missions (except for the Methodists), led by the CMS (Anglican) and conservatives, opposed the "new" orthography, while the government, the Roman Catholic and Methodist missions adopted it. Thus the old came to be dubbed

---

[27] Louis Nnamdi Oraka, *The Foundations of Igbo Studies* (Onitsha: University Publishing Company, 1983 pp. 32, 33.

"CMS" orthography and the new the "Roman Catholic" orthography.[28]

A year later, in 1930, an advisory committee that included members of the missions agreed to set up a Translation Bureau at Umuahia. In 1933, **Omenuko**, by Pita Nwana, was published after winning an all-Africa literary contest in indigenous African languages organized by the International Institute of African Languages and Culture. Nwana was the first Igbo to publish fiction in the Igbo language. The first edition was in the Protestant Orthography, but it was soon issued in the other orthographies. In 1963 Longman Nigeria published an "Official Orthography Edition" transliterated by J. O. Iroaganachi. See Ernest Emenyonu's **The Rise of the Igbo Novel** (Ibadan: Oxford University Press, 1978). In 1939, A research expedition led by Dr. Ward, to examine some dialects for possible use as a widely-accepted literary medium. She thought this might form the basis of a growing "standard" Igbo. Her "central" Igbo covered Owerri and Umuahia areas with special inclination toward Ohuhu dialect. It was gradually accepted by missionaries, writers, publishers, and Cambridge University.[29]

In 1944, Adams arranged a series of three meetings to urge the adoption of both Ward's "central' dialect and the new orthography. The first meeting was in Umuahia dated 6/13/44, attended by 24 scholars, teachers, missionaries, and government officials. Its recommendations included acceptance of Ward's

---

[28] Louis Nnamdi Oraka, *The Foundations of Igbo Studies* (Onitsha: University Publishing Company, 1983 pp. 30, 34.
[29] Louis Nnamdi Oraka, *The Foundations of Igbo Studies* (Onitsha: University Publishing Company, 1983 pp. 33, 35.

alphabet from the **Ibo Dialects and the Development of a Common Language**. The reactions and results from that meeting was that: Anglicans stuck to the Union, Catholics insisted on the Onitsha dialect, Methodists embraced central dialect. Between June 26 and 27th of the same year, the Assistant Director of Education at Enugu convened another meeting at Onitsha, attended by 27 persons from the above groups. All interest groups again stuck to their ideal dialects. On Sept. 6 of the same year, another meeting, at Enugu, attended by 16 persons, presided over by the Assistant Director of Education. It resolved that the "central" dialect would be compulsory only for literature connected with government.[30]

Four years later, in 1948, The Owerri Diocese of the Roman Catholic Mission was carved out of Onitsha Ecclesiastical Province, giving impetus to the RCM's growing practice of issuing readers in the two dialects of Onitsha and Central. But CMS, while accepting Central dialect which Ward saw as her "Union Igbo" under another name, resolved never to adopt the new orthography.[31]

The Emergence of The SPILC (1948-1972)
The same year, in 1948, Frederick Chidozie Ogbalu, mission tutor at Dennis Memorial Grammar School, Onitsha, wrote a lengthy article in the Onitsha newspaper **The Nigerian Spokesman**, challenging the new orthography. Principal E. D. C. Clark of the DMGS reprimanded him for its nationalist flavor, a sensitive

---

[30] Louis Nnamdi Oraka, *The Foundations of Igbo Studies* (Onitsha: University Publishing Company, 1983 pp. 35, 36.
[31] Louis Nnamdi Oraka, *The Foundations of Igbo Studies* (Onitsha: University Publishing Company, 1983 p. 36.

issue. Clark recommended that he produce books in Igbo to convince people that the old orthography was best. A year later, in 1949, after his transfer to St. Augustine's Grammar School, Nkwerre, Ogbalu used an existing association he had formed (Society for Promoting African Heritage) as a nucleus for the Society for Promoting Igbo Language and Culture (SPILC). One of his purposes was to fight the new orthography. Membership was at first limited to staff and students of St. Augustine's, but through its activities it was soon making an impact on Igbo people and led to a great turning point in the development of Igbo Studies.[32]

In 1950, Society for Promoting Igbo Language and Culture (SPILC) was formally inaugurated by a large percentage of the few educated Igbo men meeting at Dennis Memorial Grammar School chemistry lab, Onitsha. Officers appointed were Dr. Akanu Ibiam (President); Dr. S. E. Onwu (First Vice President); Bishop John Cross Anyogu (Second Vice President); Mr. D. C. Erinne (Chairman); F. C. Ogbalu (Secretary). The Central dialect was seen as an attempt to impose the white man's will. A new battle line was drawn between Government, RCM, and Methodist Mission on one side and SPILC and CMS on the other. SPILC acquired a public character.[33]

---

[32] Louis Nnamdi Oraka, *The Foundations of Igbo Studies* *(Onitsha: University Publishing Company, 1983 p. 36, 41.*

[33] Louis Nnamdi Oraka, *The Foundations of Igbo Studies* *(Onitsha: University Publishing Company, 1983 pp. 36, 37, 41, 42.*

By the early fifties, precisely 1952, many patriotic Igbo worried about unresolved orthography question. The Government convened another conference at Aba. Mr. R. I. Uzoma, Eastern Nigeria Minister of Education, presided. SPILC strongly opposed the "new" orthography. No decision was reached. A year later, in August 25, 1953, a select committee, chaired by Dr. S. E. Onwu, met at Owerri to reach a compromise on an orthography. The four phonetic symbols in the new orthography were removed, but the suggestion to replace them with diacritical marks was rejected. All parties except SPILC were either satisfied or no longer interested in contesting the issue. In 1954, another committee meeting, headed by Mr. Alvan Ikoku. SPILC presented a "modified" orthography. It was rejected. SPILC members walked out on the meeting. In 1955, F. C. Ogbalu issued his "compromise" orthography. So many other suggested orthographies were issued at different times by different groups and individuals. Controversy lingered until 1961, when the Government set up another committee, the Onwu Orthography Committee, chaired by Dr. S. E. Onwu, Assistant Director of Medical Services for Eastern Nigeria.[34]

Finally, in September 13, 1961, eleven members of the Onwu Committee met at the W.T.C., Enugu. The Minister of Education warned them to reconsider use of diacritical marks, in line with SPILC recommendations. They produced a pacifying orthography using diacritical marks to distinguish "light" and "heavy' vowels

---

[34] Louis Nnamdi Oraka, *The Foundations of Igbo Studies* *(Onitsha: University Publishing Company, 1983 p. 39.*

which, with other recommendations, brought to an end the 32-year-old controversy. All parties were satisfied.[35]

In June, 1962, the Government ordered all school principals to see that tutors and students acquainted themselves with the new orthography as the official Igbo orthography. The order reads: "All must use it henceforth in the teaching and studying of the language."[36]

The Standard Igbo Period (1972 - Present)

In 1972, Society for Promoting Igbo Language and Culture (SPILC) set up its Standardization Committee. Its main objectives were to adopt words from different dialects of Igbo, whether or not they belonged to the "Central" dialect areas, for the purpose of enriching the Igbo language. It was also liberal with the adoption of loan words where there were no Igbo equivalents. Thus, Standard or Modern Igbo was designed to be spoken and understood by all, because it was more flexible than Isuama, Union or "Central" dialect. It was a cross-pollination and diffusion of dialects.[37]

A year later, in August, 1973, SPILC approved the recommendation of its Standardization Committee about the spelling of Igbo words. The following year, in 1974, by intensive

---

[35] Louis Nnamdi Oraka, *The Foundations of Igbo Studies* (Onitsha: University Publishing Company, 1983 pp. 34, 40.

[36] Louis Nnamdi Oraka, *The Foundations of Igbo Studies* (Onitsha: University Publishing Company, 1983 p. 40.

[37] Louis Nnamdi Oraka, *The Foundations of Igbo Studies* (Onitsha: University Publishing Company, 1983 p. 56.

lobbying, SPILC brought about the establishment of the Dept. of Igbo Language and Culture at Alvan Ikoku College of Education. And in August, 1976, SPILC recommended the rearrangement of Igbo alphabet. In 1978, the Department of Igbo Language and Culture was started, with the opening of Anambra State College of Education at Awka, with F. C. Ogbalu as Head of Department. In September, another Department of Igbo was established at Federal Advanced Teachers College, Okene, Kwara State.[38]

Nonetheless, till date Mazi Ọnwụ committee remains the widely accepted and used orthography in Igbo language. It is the orthography used in writing this book. The challenge for computer users with Mazị Ọnwụ orthography is that, there is curremtly no Microsoft insert symbol that has both diacritic mark together with tonal mark for letters of Igbo alphabet.

Please note that the above series of events leading up to Onwu Committee of 1961 Orthography were extracted and coined from "*A History of the Igbo Language*" compiled by Frances W. Pritchett whose research on Louis Nnamdi Oraka, "*The Foundations of Igbo Studies*" helped put forward a summarized post on Columbia University website.[39]

The Ọnwụ Committee of 1961 Orthography alphabet and pronunciation as modified with revision of four letters to include 1976 Igbo Standardization Committee version which substituted c, ñ, ö and ü in Ọnwụ's orthography with ch, ṅ, ọ, ụ, are as follows:

---

[38] Louis Nnamdi Oraka, *The Foundations of Igbo Studies (Onitsha: University Publishing Company, 1983 pp. 46, 47, 48.*
[39] http://www.columbia.edu/itc/mealac/pritchett/00fwp/igbo/igbohistory.html

Letter	Pronunciation IPA
A B Ch D E F G Gb	/a/ /b/ /t͡ʃ/ /d/ /e/ /f/ /g/ /g͡b/
Gh Gw H I Ị J K Kp	/ɣ/ /gʷ/ /ɦ/ /i/ /ɪ/ /d͡ʒ/ /k/ /k͡p/
Kw L M N Nw Ny Ṅ O	/kʷ/ /l/ /m/ /n/ /ŋ/ /ŋʷ/ /ɲ/ /o/
Ọ P R S Sh T U Ụ	/ɔ/ /p/ /ɹ/ /s/ /ʃ/ /t/ /u/ /ʊ/
V W Y Z	/v/ /w/ /j/ /z/

The IPA (International Phonetic Alphabet) uses collection of characters to transcribe any human voice sound, from various languages of the world, in a way that people skilled in foreign languages and language enthusiasts across the globe can understand, regardless of their mother language or cultural background.

Divisions of Alphabet (Nkeji nke Abiidii Igbo dị ụzọ abụọ):

1. Ụdaụme (vowel)
2. Mgbochiume (consonants)

Ụdaụme (Vowels): Unlike English language, there are eight vowels that make up the Igbo vowels. The letters that make up the Igbo vowels are:

a   e   i   o   u   ị   ọ   ụ

Igbo vowels are divided into Ụdamfe (Light vowels) and Ụdaarọ (Heavy vowels):

ỤDAMFE (Light Vowel):   e   i   o   u

ỤDAARỌ (Heavy Vowel):   a   ị   ọ   ụ

Ụdamfe (Light vowels) are vowels that do not have dot under the letters and include the letter 'e'; on the other hand, Ụdaarọ (Heavy vowels) are vowels with dot under the letters and include 'a'.

ỤDAMFE (Light Vowel):   e   I   o   u

ỤDAARỌ (Heavy Vowel):   a   ị   ọ   ụ

Mgbochiume (Consonants): there are twenty-eight consonants in Igbo Alphabet. The letters that make up the consonants in Igbo alphabet are:

b	ch	d	f	g	gb	gh	gw
h	j	k	kp	kw	l	m	n
ṅ	nw	ny	p	r	s	sh	t
v	w	y	z.				

The Igbo consonants are divided into two, namely mgbochiume mgị (ordinary consonants), and Mgbochiume mkpi (diagraphs).

Mgbochiume mgị (consonant of "gị" sound): These are consonants that are not Mgbochiume mkpi (diagraphs). There are nineteen letters that make up the consonant of "gị" sound which are:

b	d	f	g	h	j	k	l
m	n	ṅ	p	r	s	t	v
w	y	z.					

Mgbochiume mkpị (Diagraphs): These are consonants that are a combination of two consonant letters. There are two Latin consonants that form single letters in Igbo language. There are nine digraphs in Igbo alphabet. These are:

ch gb   gh   gw   kp   kw   nw   ny   sh

It is of great importance to always remember that despite digraphs such as ch, gh, gb, kp, kw, and sh, do not count as double consonants and pronounced as a single sound.

Syllabic consonant (Ndagba Myiriụdaume)
A syllable is a unit of pronunciation having one vowel sound, with or without surrounding consonants, forming the whole or a part of a word; e.g., there are two syllables in *often*, three in *napkin* and one in *book*. Syllables usually contain a vowel and accompanying consonants.

There are two types of syllabic consonants: syllabic consonants and non-syllabic consonants.

A syllabic consonant or vocalic consonant is a consonant that forms a syllable on its own, like the m, n and l in the English or m and n in Igbo language. A Syllabic Consonant in Igbo language are the two prominent pseudo-vowels also known as semi-vowel. The two vowels can replace the vowel in a syllable and produce a meaningful shorter syllable or word. They make it possible to make some short syllables shorter and simpler. For example: *ama* (neighbourhood) replacing /a/ with /m/ will become *mma* (beauty).

M and N are the only syllabic nasal consonants in Igbo language. The rest of igbo consonants are non-syllabic. They cannot be seen sitting next to themselves in an Igbo word. Like in the example above, *mma* is a word but there is no such thing as *bba* in Igbo language. The same applies to the rest of the non-syllabic consonants.

Syllabic consonants harmony (Ndagba myiriudaume): this refers to rules that apply when syllabic consonants and non-syllabic are combined together in words. It is a grammatical rule that all Igbo consonants follow when forming a word with a syllabic nasal consonant "m" and "n" in word spelling. The consonant that are allowed to combine with "m" are different from the consonants that "n" combines with.

"M"syllabic nasal harmony:
The syllabic nasal harmony rule shows that consonants that are allowed to combined with syllabic nasal consonant "m" are consonants that belong to Labial Velar (Mkpọnegbugbere Ọnụ) and labiodental (Mkpọnegbugbere Ọnụ na Eze). For example: b, f, gb, kp, m, p, v, w and y.

| **Word** | **Meaning** | **Word** | **Meaning** |
| Mbe | Tortoise | Mbughari | Carry Around |

Mfe	Simple	Mfepụ	Fly out
Mgbe	When	Mgbaaka	Bracelet
Mkpuchi	Coverup	Mkpo	Vessel/container
Mkpu	Shout	Mma	Beauty
Mmadu	Human	Mpiputa	Press Out
Mpụta	Emergence	Mpio	Narrow door
Mvọ isi	Comb	mvọcha	Scrape out
Mwuli	Motivation	Mwetu	Demoralization
Mwapo	Creep up	Mwepu	Subtraction
Myọ	Sieve	Myocha	Investigate

"N" syllabic nasal harmony:

The syllabic nasal harmony rule shows that consonants that are allowed to combine with syllabic nasal consonant "n" are consonants that belong to Alveolar (Mkpọnanyụrụ na Akpo), Palatoaveolar (Mkpọnakpo ihu na akpo ime), Velar (Mkpọnegbugbere Ọnụ na Akpo) and Glottal (Mkpọekoapiri). For example: ch, d, g, gh, gw, h, j, k, kw, l, ṅ, n, nw, ny, r, s, sh, t, and z.

Word	Meaning	Word	Meaning
Ncha	Soap	Nche	Security
Nde	Million	Ndụ	Life
Nge	Singular Item	Nghaghari	Stiring
Ngwaa	Verb	Njụ	Salad dressing
Njepụ	Outdoor walks	Nhọpụta	Choosing
Njem	Journey	Nkewa	Separate
Nkịta	Dog	Nkwọ	A Market Day
Nlocha	Devour	Nna	Father
Nne	Mother	Nñomi	Emulate
Nnyetu	Share	Nrọ	Dream

Nshịpụ	Slippery	Nso	Holy
Nta	Hunnting	Ntọhapụta	Liberation
Nzapu	Sweep Out	Nzọpụta	Salvation

ADVANCED IGBO LANGUAGE

Chapter 3

Igbo Alphabet (Mkpụrụedemede Igbo)

Letters of Igbo Alphabet

There are thirty-six letters in Igbo alphabet. Igbo alphabet is called in Igbo language Abịịdịị Igbo. The Abịịdịị Igbo used in this book is from Igbo Izugbe which is the central Igbo from Mazị Ọnwụ Committee. It has two forms: capital and small letters. See examples below.

Akara ukwu (capital letter):
A   B   CH   D   E   F   G   GB   GH   GW   H   I
Ị   J   K   KP   KW   L   M   N   Ṅ   NW   NY   O
Ọ   P   R   S   SH   T   U   Ụ   V   W   Y   Z

Akara nta (small letter)
a   b   ch   d   e   f   g   gb   gh   gw   h   i   ị   j   k   kp
kw   l   m   n   ṅ   nw   ny   o   ọ   p   r   s   sh   t   u
ụ   v   w   y   z

Igbo Alphabet and Their Inclusive Words

A	Aka (Hand)	M	Mmiri (Water)
B	Bọọlu (Ball)	N	Nkịta (dog)
CH	Chịnchị (Bedbug)	Ṅ	Nụọ (Drink)
D	Dee (Write)	NW	Nwa (Baby)
E	Enyi (Elephant)	NY	Nye (Give)
F	Fe (fly)	O	Osisi (Tree)
G	Gụọ (read)	Ọ	Ọka (Corn)
GB	Gbanye (Pour)	P	Pọpọ (Papaya)
GH	Ghe (fry)	R	Rie (eat)
GW	Gwa (Tell)	S	Saa (Wash)
H	Hụọ (Roast)	SH	Ịsha (Crab)
I	Ite (Pot)	T	Torotoro (Turkey)
Ị	Ịgba (Drum)	U	Unere (Banana)
J	Ji (Yam)	Ụ	Ụlọ (House)
K	Iko (Cup)	V	Mvọ isi (Comb)
KP	Kpakpando (Star)	W	Kụwaa (Break)
KW	Kwụọ (Grind)	Y	Ịnyịnya (Horse)
L	Leta (Letter)	Z	Azịza (Broom)

Vowels and Consonants

Divisions of Alphabet (Nkeji nke Abiidii Igbo dị ụzọ abụọ):
1. Ụdaụme (vowel)
2. Mgbochiume (consonants)

UDAUME (Vowels)

Ụdaụme (Vowels): Unlike English language, there are eight vowels that make up the Igbo vowels. The letters that make up the Igbo vowels are:

a e i o u ị ọ ụ

Igbo vowels are divided into Ụdamfe (Light vowels) and Ụdaarọ (Heavy vowels):

ỤDAMFE (Light Vowel):   e   I   o   u

ỤDAARỌ (Heavy Vowel):   a   ị   ọ   ụ

Ụdamfe (Light vowels) are vowels that do not have dot under the letters and includes the letter 'e'; on the other hand, Ụdaarọ (Heavy vowels) are vowels with dot under the letters and include 'a'.

ỤDAMFE (Light Vowel):   e   I   o   u

ỤDAARỌ (Heavy Vowel):   a   ị   ọ   ụ

Vowel Harmony (Ndakorita udaume Igbo)
Vowel harmony applies to heavy and light vowels syllabic combination in words. It is a grammatical rule that Ụdamfe (Light vowels) usually consist of vowels of its own syllables (such as e, i, o and u) in a word. They do not combine with Ụdaarọ (heavy vowel: a, ị, ọ and ụ) unless it is a compound verb or word.

Translation to Igbo
Ụdamfe na ụdaarọ anaghi anoko onụ na otu mkpụrụ okwu. O bụrụ na ụdamfe di na mkpụrụ okwu ọ bụ nani mkpuru uda ya puru ịdị na mkpụrụ okwu ahụ na otu aka ahu ka ọ dị kwa na ụdaarọ. Nke a ka anakpọ iwu na achị ụdamfe na ụdaarọ.

Ọmụmaatụ:
Ụdamfe: Osisi (Tree), Iko (cup), Ukwe (song) etc.
Ụdaarọ: Ụlọ (house). Ụka (church), Ọka (corn) etc.

Types of Vowels Sounds in Igbo Syllable (Ụdịdị Mkpọpụta ụdaume na Nkejiokwu Igbo)

There are two types of vowels in the Igbo syllable namely: monophthong and diphthong.

Monophthong (Ụdange): Monophthong also known as short vowel (ụdaume di nkenke) is a vowel that is spoken with exactly one tone and one mouth position. It is a single vowel articulated without change in quality throughout the course of a syllable. It is the only vowel sound produced in a word and it does not require other vowels to support in the production of sound of words that it is a part of.

Example of monophthong is as follows:

Word	Monophthong	~ in a Sentence
Chaa	aa	Chaa n'ụzọ ahụ dị njọ. *Avoid that bad road*
Chọọ	ọọ	Chọọ ewu ojii ahụ. *Find the black goat.*
Dọọ	ọọ	Dọọ ụmụ gị aka na ntị. *Warn your children.*
Kpeenụ	ee	Kpeenụ ya n'aka nne ya *Report him to her mom*
Kpọọrọ	ọọ	Kpọọrọ m ya n'ekwentị

		Call him on the phone
Kweere	ee	Dinta ahụ kweere ọnya.
		The hunter set his trap
Meere	ee	O meere ha ihe ọma.
		She did him/her a favor.
Mgbaaka	aa	Mgbaaka Ada dị ọcha.
		Ada's bracelet is clean.
Mịịrị	ịị	Osisi ahụ mịịrị mkpụrụ.
		That tree has fruits.

Diphthong (Ụdamkpị):

This is a sound formed by the combination of two vowels in a single syllable, in which the sound begins as one vowel and moves toward another (as in coin, loud, and side). It is a sound that is made up of two separate vowel sounds within the same syllable.

It is important to note that having two consecutive letters especially consonants do not result into a diphthong. Igbo consonants do not function as a diphthong and they do not occur side by side in Igbo words. The only exception to this rule is semi—vowels which double as Igbo consonants. The alphabet (m, n) or sounds /m, n/ are permitted to reduplicate in a word, e.g. mma, nna, nne, nnu, mmadụ and so on.

There are six types of Igbo diphthong but there are eight in English language. The six types of Igbo diphthong are: ụọ, io, ie, uo, iọ and ịa. These diphthongs can be separated into *preceding* and *ending* diphthongs.

The *preceding vowels* refer to those vowel sounds that produced first in the pronunciation of diphthongs. There are four *preceding diphthong vowels* in Igbo language and they are: /ị/, /i/, /ụ/ and /u/.

The *ending vowels* refer to those vowel sounds that produced first in the pronunciation of diphthongs. There are four *ending diphthong vowels* in Igbo language and they are: /a/, /e/, /o/ and /ọ/.

Example of the six types of diphthongs in Igbo language are as follows:

Word	Monophthong	~ in a Sentence
Hio	io	Ha Hio ya ụkwara ahụ.
		They infected him with cough.
Hịochapụ	ịọ	Hịochapụ ya ọnụ ọjọọ.
		Deal with his arrogant words.
kpụọrọ	ụọ	Kpụọrọ ya Ụlọ aja.
		Build (form) a sand castle for him
Merie	ie	Merie onye owụwa ahụ.
		Overcome the tempter
Pịata	ịa	Pịara ya otito ahụ.
		Poop his bump/pimple.
Tigbuo	uo	Tigbuo ndị iro gị.
		Crush your enemies.

Vowel Assimilation (Olilo udaume):
Assimilation is a sound change, where some phonemes (typically consonants or vowels) change to more similar other nearby sounds. This happens during rapid speed pronunciation of two words.

For example:
> I don't know   /I duno/
> Camera   /kamra/

And this omission is often indicated in print by an apostrophe. For example: 'fish 'n' chips'.

In Igbo language, vowel Assimilation (Olilo udaume) is the process whereby two vowels of two words sitting beside each other harmonize and pronounce with one sound as though it was one vowel present in those compound words.

Igbo translation of the above definition: *Olilo ụdaume bụ otu ụdaume si eme ka udaume nodebere ya yie ya na mkpọpụta mkpụrụokwu abụọ nọdebere onwe ha.*

Examples:

English	Igbo (Normal)	Assimilation
Boss/Leader	Onye + isi	onyiisi
Health	Ahụ + ike	Ahiike
Peacemaker/seeker	Ọchọ + udo	Ọchuudo
Strong hand	Aka + ike	akiike
Welldone	jisi + ike	jiisike

During Vowel Assimilation, two words that have two vowels sitting beside each other experience a dropping of one: the condition is that the vowel which is "stronger" (greater pitch sound) will overide the sound pronunciation of the "weaker" (lower pitch sound) vowel sound before it.

There are five kinds of vowel Assimilation (Olilo udaume) in Igbo language. They are:
1. Progressive Assimilation (Olilo ihu)
2. Regressive Assimilation (Olilo azụ)
3. Coalescent Assimilation (Olilo mmakọ)
4. Conditional Assimilation (Olilo ndapụta)
5. Complete Assimilation (Olilo nlocha)

Progressive Assimilation (Olilo Ihu):
Forward dropping happens when the first word ending in a vowel pitch overides the second word's first vowel, thereby replacing the vowel with its own vowel. It is uncommon to notice progressive assimiliation unlike regressive assimiliation.

Igbo translation: *A na-enwe olilo ihu mgbe nke mbụ gara n'ihu loo ụdaume dị n'okwu nke abụọ we me onwe ka ọ bụrụ ụdaime ahụ.*

It can be expressed in the form of:
Preceding vowel + Following Vowel = Preceding vowel reduplication.

$$V_P + V_F = V_P V_P \text{ if } V_F \text{ is /a/}$$

For example:

Words	Merging of Elements	Pronunciation
eju + a	eju a	eju u
ekwe + a	ekwe a	ekwe e
elu + a	elu a	elu u
esu +a	esu a	esu u
nzu a	nzu a	nzu u
obe a	obe a	obe e
ogbe a	Ogbe a	ogbe e

oge + a   oge a   oge e

Regressive Assimilation (Olilo Azụ): Forward dropping happens when the first vowel of the second outrides the sound pitchword of the first ending vowel pitch.

Igbo translation: *A na-enwe olilo azụ mgbe ụdaume bidoro okwu nke abụọ loo mkpụrụokwu kwwụsịrị ụdaume nke mbụ.*

It can be expressed in the form of:
Preceding vowel + Following Vowel = Following vowel reduplication.
$V_P + V_F = V_F V_F$ if V_F is /a, e, o, ọ/

Compounnd word	*Merged*	*Pronunciation*
Nwa + eke	nweeke	nweke
Oke + anu	okaanu	okanu
Ada + obi	adoobi	adobi
Uso + ekwu	useekwu	usekwu
Ego + ọkụ	Egọọkụ	Egọkụ
Ome + ire	Omiire	Omire

Coalescent Assimilation (Olilo mmakọ): This process causes a sound to change by merging two contiguous vowel sounds (invariably adjacent) into another vowel sound different from the two coalesced sounds. This is usually the case when two words are pronounced with rapid speed.

This kind of assimilation often happens when that last word that is merging with the first word is the Igbo word "ya." The third person reflective or object pronoun "ya" would drop the consonant

/y/ to either use the vowel /a/ or /e/. Otherwise, it would leave the word "ya" and change the vowel preceding it, "ya" or both the preceding vowel and the vowel after /y/.

It can be expressed in the following forms:

FORM 1: When "Following" vowel is any vowel of the same tone and vowel group (harmony) of /i/ or /ị/, the /i/ or /ị/ is substituted with the consonant "y" whose phoneme is /j/.

V_P = Preceding vowel and V_F = Following vowel
$V_P + V_F = \text{'y'}V_S$

Notice the introduction of 'y' is the phoneme /j/ as a replacement for V_P.

For example:

Compound words	Merging words	Coalescent A.
asị and ọcha	asị + ọcha	asyọcha
lie and white	*lie + white*	*white lie*
ụdịrị and azụ	ụdịrị + azụ	ụdịryazụ
Type and fish	*type + fish*	*type of fish*
enyi and oma	enyi + oma	enyyoma
friend and good	*friend + good*	*good friend*
ezi and omume	ezi + omume	ezyomume
good and behavior	*good + behavior*	*good behavior*

Notice the vowel harmony and the de-syllabification that is accompanied by the substitution of /i/ or /ị/ with consonant "y" whose grapheme is /j/.

FORM 2: When "Following is the pronoun "ya", the consonant "y" whose approximant is /j/, will drop out and the vowel "a" would remain or change following vowel harmony rule in terms of heavy or light vowel. The Igbo word "ya" is the pronoun for his, her, it or its in English.

V_P = Preceding vowel and "ya" = Following vowel
V_P + ya = ịya (heavy vowel)
V_P + ya = iye (light vowel)

Heavy vowel (Ụdaarọ):   a   ị   ọ   ụ
Light vowel (Ụdamfe):   e   i   o   u

For example:

Compound words	Coalescent A.	Vowel type
afọ + ya	afịya	heavy
aka + ya	akịya	heavy
akwa + ya	akwịya	heavy
anya + ya	anyịya	heavy
azụ + ya	azịya	heavy
ego + ya	egiye	light
ije + ya	ijiye	light
ike + ya	ikiye	light
imi + ya	imiye	light
mkpa + ye	mkpịya	heavy
ntị + ya	ntịya	heavy
nwanne + ya	nwanniye	light

oche + ya	ochiye	light
ọnụ + ya	ọnịya	heavy
uche + ya	uchiye	light
ụda + ya	ụdịya	heavy

Conditional Assimilation (Olilo ndapụta): This type of assimilation does not occur unless there is a rapid pronunciation of words. In the absence of rapid speed, there is no assimilation.

It can be expressed in the following forms:

FORM 1: When "Preceding" vowel is /u/ or /ụ/, the /u/ or /ụ/ is eclipsed by the "Following" vowel; which make the preceding adopt the phonetic sound of the "Following" vowel thereby producing a reduplication form of "Following" vowel. Note that this can only occur during rapid utterance.

V_P = Preceding vowel and V_F = Following vowel

$V_P + V_F = V_F V_F$ if V_P is /u/ or /ụ/ during rapid pronunciation.

For example:

Merging words	Rapid utterance	Slow utterance
Agụ + ọhịa	Agọọhịa	Agụohịa
Leopard + Forest	*Wild Leopard*	*Wild Leopard*
Azụ + aka	Azaaka	Azụaka
Back + Hand	*back of hand*	*back of hand*
mkpụrụ + ọka	mkpụrọọka	mkpụrụọka
Seed + corn	*Corn seed*	*Corn seed*

Okwu + ego   Okweego   Okwuego
Talk + money   *Talk about money*

Ọnụ + azụ   Ọnaazụ   Ọnụazụ
Mouth + fish   *mouth of fish* *mouth of fish*

Complete Assimilation: (Olilo Nlocha): Complete assimilation happens when the preceding vowel (a, e, o and ọ) are eclipsed by the "Following" light vowel (i, e, u, o) which also reduplicates itself within the merged words.

It can be expressed in the form of:
Preceding vowel + Following Vowel = Following vowel reduplication.
V_P + V_F = $V_F V_F$ if V_P is /a, e, o, ọ/

Compounnd word   *Merged*   *Pronunciation*
Nwa + ike   nwaike   nwiike
Ude + isi   Udeisi   Udiisi
Aha + ihe   Ahaihe   Ahiihe
Ụlọ + Obi   Ụlọobi   Ụloobi
Ego + enwe   Egọenwe   Egeenwe

Vowel Elision (Ndapu Ụdaume)
Vowel Elision is the omission of a vowel sound (a phoneme) in speech. Vowel elision often occurs in the Igbo compound words. Vowel elision happens when compound words with vowel ending and beginning siting side by side are spoken together faster than normal.

Igbo translation: *Ndapụ ụdaume bụ ọpụpụ otu ọdaume na mkpọpụta ụdaume abụọ nọkọtara ọnọ.*

The following are examples of elision of vowels that affect syllables because of the same pitch level they have. This is referred to as diachronic elision because it has affected two words.

English	*Igbo (Normal)*	*Dropping*
Male/man	nwa + oke	*nwoke*
Strong man	di + ike	*dike*
Stove	uso + ekwu	*usekwu*
Doctor	Di + ibia	*dibia*

MGBOCHIUME (Consonants)

Mgbochiume (Consonants): there are twenty-eight consonants in Igbo Alphabet. The letters that make up the consonanats in Igbo alphabet are:

b	ch	d	f	g	gb	gh	gw
h	j	k	kp	kw	l	m	n
ṅ	nw	ny	p	r	s	sh	t
v	w	y	z.				

The Igbo consonants are divided into two, namely mgbochiume mgị (ordinary consonants), and Mgbochiume mkpi (diagraphs).

A. Mgbochiume mgị (consonant of "gị" sound): These are consonants that are not Mgbochiume mkpi (diagraphs). There are nineteen letters that make up the consonant of "gị" sound which are:

| b | d | f | g | h | j | k | l |

m   n   ṅ   p   r   s   t   v
w   y   z.

B. Mgbochiume mkpị (Diagraphs): These are consonants that are a combination of two consonants. There are nine digraphs in Igbo alphabet. These are:

Ch   gb   gh   gw   kp   kw   nw   ny   sh

It is of great importance to always remember that despite digraphs such as ch, gh, gb, kp, kw, and sh, do not count as double consonants and pronounced as a single sound.

Consonant Elision (Ndapu Mgbochiume)
Consonant Elision is the omission of one or more consonant sounds (a phoneme) in speech. Consonant elision often occurs in the Igbo words with multiple consonant sounds. Consonant is heard when these words with one or more consonants sounds are spoken faster than normal.

For example:
Hand bag drops (asimilates) the consonant letter /d/ when pronounced faster as *hanbag*.

Ndapu mgbochiume bu oge arapulu itinye mgbochiume ebe o kwersi idi maka na i na-akpoputa ya osiso.

English	*Normal*	*Elision*
Suffering	Afụfụ	Aụfụ
question	Ajụjụ	Aụjụ
Story	Akụkọ	Aụkọ

Side	Akụkụ	Aụkụ
Book	Akwụkwọ	Aụkwọ
Prophesy	Amụma	Aụma
Broom	Azịza	Aịza
Dress code	Ejije	Eije
Tree	Osiso	Oiso
Belief/Faith	Okwukwe	Oukwe
Chicken	Ọkụkọ	Ọụkọ
Morning	Ụtụtụ	Ụụtụ

Pseudo/Nasalized Vowels

Myiriudaume (semi-vowel, pseudo-vowels or nasalized vowel): These are consonants that are pronounced in similar manner in which vowels are pronounced. There are two letters that make up mgbochiume (nasalized vowels) and they are:

      m   and   n

The Myiriudaume (nasalized vowels) function like vowels in the words with them. Note that you cannot treat "n" as a nasalized vowel when it is in the form of diagraph, for examples: ny, nw, or ñ.

    ńnà - father
    ńné - mother
    ḿmā - good/beautiful
    ḿmà - knife

Tonal Accent Marks (Diacritics)

Tone is a pitch accent. It is used in Igbo language to show the different meaning of words though they are spelt the same. Tone performs syllabic stress and semantic function in Igbo language.

Tonal marking, also referred to as diacritical marks, are extra symbols that are placed above or below a letter to modify the pronunciation or clarify the meaning of a word. In pronunciation, tone distinguishes pitch level of a syllable. These are examples of their usage in the Igbo language:

Letter	Acute (High tone)	Macron (Mid tone)	Grave (Low tone)
a	Á á	Ā ā	À à
e	É é	Ē è	Ē ē
I	Í í	Ī ī	Ì ì
ị	Ị́ ị́	Ī ī	Ị̀ ị̀
o	Ó ó	Ō ò	Ō ō
ọ	Ọ́ ọ́	Ō ō	Ọ̀ ọ̀
u	Ú ú	Ū ū	Ù ù
ụ	Ụ́ ụ́	Ū ū	Ụ̀ ụ̀
m	Ḿ ḿ	Ṁ ṁ	Ṁ ṁ
n	Ń ń	Ṅ ṅ	Ǹ ǹ

Examples:
ákwá	-	cry	[high tone – high tone]
àkwá	-	egg	[low tone – high tone]
àkwà	-	bridge/bed	[low tone – low tone]
ákwà	-	cloth	[high tone – low tone]
ísí	-	head	[high tone – high tone]
ìsì	-	blindness	[low tone – low tone]
ísì	-	smell	[high tone – low tone]
ìsí	-	to cook	[low tone – high tone]
óké	-	male	[high tone – high tone]

òkè	-	portion	[low tone – low tone]
ókè	-	boundary	[high tone – low tone]
òké	-	rat/mouse	[low tone – high tone]
ńnà	-	father	[high tone – low tone]
ńné	-	mother	[high tone – high tone]
ḿmā	-	good	[high tone – mid tone]
ḿmà	-	knife	[high tone – low tone]

When "m" and "n" function as nasalized or pseudo-vowels in Igbo language, it means they can be expressed with tonal markings like other vowels. Therefore, they are pronounced with high, mid or low tones.

In Igbo grammar two consonants cannot follow each other unlike other languages where consonant clusters exist. As a result, "m" or "n" sitting in front of another consonant are given tonal marking which makes it function as a pseudo vowel.

Examples:
ńnà	–	father [Acute – Grave]
ńné	–	mother [Acute – Accent]
ḿmā	–	good [Acute – Macron]
ḿmà	–	knife [Acute – Grave]

If a word ends with a vowel sound, and the word after it begins with a vowel sound, then the later word with "stronger" vowel swallows the "weaker" vowel sound/the vowel sound before it.

Also, tonal marking helps to distinguish and disambiguate phrases, clauses and sentences that are otherwise similar in written expressions.

For example:
Ọ dị mmā.
It is good. (Declarative)

Ọ dị mmā?
Is it good? (Interrogative)

Ọ dị mmā
If it is good (Conditional)

Chapter 4

Spelling and spelling rules (Nsupe na Iwu Nsupe)

Spelling is the forming of words from letters according to accepted usage. Igbo language like every other language orthography has spelling rules to follow for proper spelling and writing of words. The following five spelling and writing rules apply to any formation of Igbo words.

RULE 1: *All consonants of Igbo alphabet (excluding "v" and "sh") can start a word but not end words. However, special consonants referred to as Pseudo-vowels are permitted.*

Generally, Igbo words are not allowed to end with consonants. There are twenty-eight Igbo consonants. Among these twenty-eight consonants only consonants that are pseudo-vowels are exempted from this rule. Pseudo-vowels are "m" and "n". The most used pseudo-vowel in this case is "m." The following examples reveal the exempted condition which are majorly found in few names of animals, collective noun and figures of speech.

All – dum (collective noun)
Periwinkle - Ịsam (name of animal)
Innuendo - Ikpem (figure of speech)
Hippopotamus Utobo/Akum
Lion - Ọdụm

Please be aware that most names of human beings that end with pseudo-vowels are often a phrase, clause or sentence. For example:

Chukwubuikem – *God is my strength.*
Ikem – *my strength*
Chinecherem – *My God thinks after me.*
Chidubem – *May God keeps leading me.*

RULE 2: *No Successive Use of Consonants*

Back-to-back use of consonants does not exist in Igbo words formation. When consonants are in successive form, they follow or precede one another in the same word. And since diagraphs are considered as single entities and pronounced as single letters, they do not break the rule. The following examples show that this rule is followed.

Dabere - *lean on*
Kele – *greet/thank*
Efere - *plate*
Ngajị - *spoon*
Ụlọ - *house*
Akara - *mark*
and so on

Examples with diagraphs:

Akwa –	*Egg*
Ugwu –	*Mountain*
Akwụkwọ -	*Book*
Nwatakịrị -	*Child*
Agwọ -	*Snake*

RULE 3: *All words end with Igbo vowels or pseudo-vowel.*

Igbo words in general usually end with vowels or Pseudo-vowels. There are eight Igbo vowels. Any of the eight Igbo vowels can be the last letter in Igbo words. This rule applies to Igbo nouns, verbs, adjectives, adverbs and so on. For example:

ihụnanya -	*love*
udo -	*peace*
nke onye -	*private*
ihe nzuzo -	*secret*
nchekwa -	*security*

In Igbo morphology and lexicology, words whose spelling begins with a vowel must have at least another vowel in it. As a result, Igbo words do not permit vowel – consonant – VC- syllable structure as in English language. Another significant aspect of the Igbo writing and spelling system as it regards how spelling relates to phoneme is that, all sound in writable spelling must be pronounced.

RULE 4: *Successive use of vowel is allowed.*

Back-to-back use of vowels is allowed in Igbo words formation. When vowels are in successive form, they must follow vowel harmony rule.

Vowel harmony applies to heavy and light vowels syllabic combination in words. It is a form of grammatical rule that Ụdamfe (Light vowels) usually consist of vowels of its own syllables (such as e, i, o and u) in a word. They do not combine with Ụdaarọ (heavy vowel: a, ị, ọ and ụ) unless it is a compound verb or word. Words that are imperative verbs in Igbo language often end with vowels written in a successive form. For example:

        Ndeewo - *hello*
        Nnọọ - *welcome*
        Dalụụ - *well-done*
        Lee - *look/behold*
        Ee - *yes*
        Kpọọ - *call*

RULE 5: <u>*Successive use of pseudo-vowel is allowed.*</u>

Back-to-back use of pseudo-vowels is allowed in Igbo words formation. Although "m" and "n" are part of the twenty-eight Igbo consonants, they are special consonants and are referred to as pseudo-vowels because of their vowel's characteristics. This characteristic nature gives it the preference over other consonants. The example of successive use of pseudo-vowel is as follows:

        ńnà   -   father
        ńné   -   mother
        ḿmā   -   good/beautiful

ḿmà   -   knife

RULE 6: *Pseudo-vowels preceding other consonants.*

Pseudo-vowels that precede fellow consonants in the formation of Igbo words are allowed to do so in the following two ways:

Sub-rule 1: Pseudo-vowel "m" must be ahead of the following nine consonants: b, f, gb, m, p, kp, v, w, y.

Sub-rule 2: Pseudo-vowel "n" must be ahead of the remaining nineteen consonants:

ch	d	g	gh	gw	h	j	k	kw
l	n	ṅ	nw	ny	r	s	sh	t
z								

Examples with pseudo-vowel "m":

Mbara/Akiri – *Cricket*   Mbe - *Tortoise*
Mbuzu/Mgbaja/Nte – *Antelope*   Mfe - *Easy/Light*
Mgbada – *Antelope*   Mgbakọ - *Addition*
Mkpụrụ - *Seed*   Mma - *Knife*
Mpe - *Little/Small*   Mvọ - *Nail/Comb*
Mwepu – *Subtraction*   Myọ - *Sieve/Colander*

Examples with pseudo-vowel "n":

Ncha – *soap*   Nche – *security*
Ndida – *slope*   Ndidi – *patience*
Ngalaba – *branch*   Nganga – *pride*

Nhata – *equality* Nhọpụta – *selection*
Njikọ - *union* Nkọ - *sharp*
Nku – *wing* Nchara – *Rust*
Nchị - *Grass cutter* Nduru – *Dove*
Ngwere – *Lizard* Nkapị/Nkakwụ - *Shrew*
Nkịta Ọhịa – *Wolf* Nkwọ - *Kite*
Nshịkọ - *Crab* Nyanwuruede – *Fox*

RULE 7: *Construction and usage of "na" in written sentence.*

In Igbo language "na" when used as a conjunction or preposition follows a specific construct that indicates what part of speech it expresses.

Subrule 1: when "na" is used in a sentence to express conjunction, it is written in full. Conjunction is a part of speech that connects words, phrases, clauses or sentences. For example:

(a). Anyanwụ na Ọnwa *Sun and Moon*
(b). Ji na Ede *Yam and cocoyam*
(c). Garri na Ofe dị ụtọ. *Garri and soup is sweet*
(d) Ama m na ọ gara ahia *I know he/she went to market*
(e). Echere m na ha bi ebe a. *I thought they live here.*

Subrule 2: when "na" is used in a sentence to express preposition, which is followed by a vowel, there is omission of the vowel "a" as it becomes unstressed vowel allowing the vowel following it to take preeminence. The "na" is expressed as n'. For example:

(a). Mmiri zoro n'ụtụtụ *It rained in the morning*
(b). Ọjị dị n'ime akpa *Kola nut is in the bag*

(c). Nduru bere n'elu osisi.   *Dove perched on the tree*
(d) Isi akwụ dara n'ala   *Palm Kernel fell (to the ground)*
(e). Ada no n'ulo akwụkwọ.   *Ada is at school.*

Subrule 3: when "na" is used in a sentence to express preposition, which is followed by a consonant, there is no omission of the vowel "a" as it remains stressed vowel in the sentence. The "na" is written in full as "na". For example:

(a). Mmiri zoro na mgbede   *It rained in the evening*
(b). Azụ bi na mmiri   *Fishes live in water*
(c). Zitara m ha na chi ọbụbọ   *Send them early (morning)*
(d) Isi akwụ dabara na nkata   *Palm Kernel fell into the basket*

Chapter 5

Linguistic Ambiguity in Igbo Language (Mgbagwoju Anya di n'Asụsụ Igbo)

Linguistic ambiguity is a quality inherent in human language that makes either or both written text or spoken words open to multiple interpretations. It is that quality semantic relation that deals with various uses of words or phrases and their different meanings that makes the meaning difficult or impossible for a person or computer program to reliably decode without some additional information.

In Igbo language, there are five sources of linguistic ambiguities namely: anaphoric statement, lexical ambiguity, phonological ambiguity, structural ambiguity and ambiguity resulting from dialectal differences.

(A). Anaphoric statement: This often refers to statements that contain anaphoric pronouns. Anaphoric pronouns are used to refer to a person, objects in a text or situation in which they are uttered. It is a pronoun that points back to another word, phrase or

constituent in a sentence. A word that gets its meaning from a preceding word or phrase is also called an anaphor.

In English language, anaphoric pronouns consist of third person personal pronouns e.g. he, him, she, her, its, they, them. Third person anaphoric possessive pronouns in English language include: his, her, hers, its, their, theirs and the third person anaphoric reflexive pronouns are: himself, herself, itself, and themselves. The demonstrative pronouns include: this, that, these, those. Relative pronouns are: who, whom, which, whose for both singular and plural forms. However, the pronouns of first and second person singular and plural are usually in a deictic manner.

Unlike other language, in Igbo language, pronouns are not gendered as a result the same pronouns are used for male, female and inanimate beings. There are four singular pronouns (i, ị, o, and ọ) and two impersonal pronouns (a and e).

Every Igbo pronoun stands alone in a sentence. They do not join to verb or noun except if they are in prefixed form, as in the case of first person singular and third person plural. The following are examples of standalone and prefixed forms of Igbo pronouns:

First person singular	Igbo
I went to market.	Ejere m ahia. ("m" refers to "I")
I asked a question.	Ajuru m ajuju. ("m" refers to "I")

3rd person plural	Igbo
They did the dishes	Asara ha efere. ("ha" refers to "They")
They cooked food	Esiri ha nri. ("ha" refers to "They")

The following examples show first person singular and third person plural in their anaphoric ambiguity form.

First person singular Igbo
I went to market.   Ejere ahia. ("m" omitted)
I asked a question.   Ajuru ajuju. ("m" omitted)

3rd person plural   *Igbo*
They did the dishes   Asara efere.("ha" omitted)
They cooked food   Esiri nri. ("ha" omitted)

Also, expressions using third person singular pronoun can produce linguistic ambiguity when the subject gender, name or other identity is not revealed. This is because the personal pronoun "ọ" lacks gender and direct identity to a person or thing. See the examples below:

3rd person singular   *Igbo*
She is so beautiful   Ọ maka/ ọ mara ezigbo mma
He is handsome   Ọ maka/ ọ mara ezigbo mma
It is so beautiful   Ọ mara ezigbo mma

Notice that the pronoun "ọ" were used in place of a person as well as thing. This would pose a problem in a situation where there is no extra expression that states what or who the pronoun was referring to. For example:

English   *Igbo language*
Ada said that she is so beautiful.   Ada sị na ọ mara ezigbo mma
Ada said that he is handsome.   Ada sị na ọ mara ezigbo mma

Ada said that it is so beautiful.   Ada sị na ọ mara ezigbo mma

(B). *Lexical Ambiguities:* Lexical ambiguity is caused when two or more words have the same form (homonymy or homophony) or when a word has more than one meaning (polysemy). It is also the existence of multiple meaning of sentences due to words that have more than one meaning in that sentence. A classic example of lexical ambiguity involves the word(s) close, tear, produce, *bank*, etc.

1. They were too *close* to the door to *close* it.
2. Upon seeing the *tear* in her painting she shed a *tear*.
3. The bandage was *wound* around the *wound*.
4. The farm was cultivated to *produce produce*.
5. You must be *present* to *present* your *present* to the couple.
6. I went to the *bank*.
7. The fisherman went to the *bank*.

The simplest explanation we can give for each of these words: *Homophones* are words that sound the same but are different. *Homographs* are words that are spelled the same but are different. *Homonyms* often appear to be the difficult ones. This is because, it can be *homophones, homographs,* or both.

Ten examples of Lexical ambiguity in Igbo language:

1. abụ can refer to: *poem* or *armpit*
2. agba can refer to: *jaw* or *arthritis, appointment*
3. agwa can refer to: *beans* or *character*
4. akwa can refer to: *bridge* or *bed*
5. anwụ can refer to: *sunshine* or *mosquito*

6. ara can refer to: *madness* or *breast*
7. igwe can refer to: *iron* or *bicycle*
8. igwe can refer to: *king* or *sky*
9. ilu can refer to: *proverb* or *bitterness*
10. ude can refer to: *fame* or *body lotion*

(C). Phonological Ambiguities: phonetics deals with sounds within a language or between different languages. In English language, phonological ambiguities occur in a sentence or expression where words that sound the same but have different meanings and can be used in very different ways are used without distinguishing elements. Here are some English language examples: buy/bye/by, too/two/to, see/sea, site/sight, right/write and so on.

Examples in English language sentences are as follows:

1. How can I *intimate* this to my most *intimate* friend?
2. I did not *object* to the *object* which he showed me.
3. I had to *subject* the *subject* to a series of questioning.
4. The dump was so full that the workers had to *refuse* more *refuse*.
5. The soldier decided to *desert* the tasty *dessert* in the desert.

In Igbo language, Homonyms (Nyiri) is among the factor of linguistic ambiguity. Homonyms may be referred to those words that have identical pronunciations and identical spellings but hold different meanings. Homonym is the ambiguous way of expressing either homophones or homograph. All homonyms are homophones because they sound the same. However, not all homophones are homonyms. Homophones with different spellings are not homonyms. Homonyms (Nyiri) is a big deal in written Igbo words as one would not have a way of knowing what is being said.

Homophones (Ụdịrị): Homophones refer to those words that have identical pronunciations but may hold different meanings or spelling. Also, it may be words that have two identical pronunciations but possess different meanings and spellings. For example: carrot, caret, and carat.

Ten examples of Homophones in English language:

1. A *site* that was chosen for the new school was denied because the city *cited* the environment factors.
2. Brian went *by* his grandmother's house to say hello and *bye* on his way to *buy* food.
3. Do not *alter* the plan to bring it to the *altar*.
4. Do you *know* that *no* fish can survive with water?
5. During his first-year *course* research, Smith could not walk on the *coarse* sand in a hot afternoon.
6. *For* your information, the doors of the airplane are located *fore* and aft and *four* things need to be taken care of before takeoff.
7. He screamed *aloud* that smoking is not *allowed*.
8. He was *billed* monthly for loan used for the *build* (house).
9. I *ate* *eight* slices of cake during the wedding.
10. I could *hear* the sound of her voice from *here*.

Homophones in Igbo language largely differ from other languages, beside numerous dialects, in that words cannot be pronounce differently from how they are spelt. Standard/central Igbo language as accepted means communication and writing does not have words that are spelt differently and pronounced the same. However, Igbo language has words that are spelled the same way but have different meanings and pronunciations.

1. *Arapụ* gị n'ụzọ; Ị ga-ama ụzọ ịlota? – if left on your own would you find your way home or if you run if you went crazy on your way would you be able to find your way home.
2. *Amụ* siri ya ike – He was born strong or his penis is strong.

Homograph (Ngakwọta): Homographs refer to those words that have identical spellings but hold different meanings and sometimes different pronunciations. The major observable distinction between homographs and homophones occurs among words with identical spelling but different pronunciation. Also, it may be words that have two identical pronunciations but possess different meanings and spellings.

(D). Structural Ambiguities: Structural ambiguity results when an utterance might have more than one grammatical structure. In English language, ambiguity may occur in the grammatical structure of phrases, clauses or sentences formation as well as expression. For example:

1. Flying planes can be dangerous.

Other examples of structural ambiguity in English language:

A. Between compound noun and a noun phrase.

- Flying object: *An object to fly/An object that flies*
- Moving car: *A car for moving/A car that moves*
- Walking stick: *A stick to walk with/A stick that walks.*

- Running board: *A board to run on/A board that runs.*

B. Structural ambiguities in sentence forms:

- *The teacher said on Friday she would give a quiz.* This sentence means either that it was on Friday that the teacher told the class about the quiz or that the quiz would be given on Friday.
- *The chicken is ready to eat.* This could mean either the chicken is cooked and can be eaten now or the chicken is ready to be fed.
- *The robbers threatened the cashiers with the guns.* This sentence either means that bank robbers armed with guns threatened cashiers or the cashiers that bank robbers threatened were holding guns.

Structural ambiguities in Igbo language is something that happens very often. This is because people often express themselves and their experiences in fewer words and abundant use of pronouns.

1. Adaobi erighi nri ya – *Adaobi didn't eat her own food or Adaobi didn't eat somebody's food.*
2. Amaka sị na Ọ ga-abịa – *Amaka said that she (Amaka) would come or Amaka said that somebody else would come.*
3. Gịnị butere gị ebe a? – *Why did you come here? Or Through what means did you come.*
4. Ọ tara anụ mmadụ -- *He/she ate meat that belongs to another person or He/she ate human flesh.*
5. Ndi nkuzi Igbo na-ama akwụkwọ -- *Teachers of Igbo*

extract are brilliant or Teachers that teach Igbo language are brilliant.

6. Onye nwe mma isi wara – *Who own the knife whose handle is broken or the owner of the knife has a broken head.*
7. Ngwere ahụ na-ata ahụhụ -- *The Lizard is eating Ants or the Lizard is suffering.*
8. Okọcha na-agba bọọlụ -- *Okọcha plays football (as career) or Okọcha is playing football (current event).*
9. Emeka na-agụ akwụkwọ -- *Emeka is a student or Emeka is reading a book (current event).*
10. Nna Ugochi and Adamma bịara taa – *Ugochi and Adamma dad came today (one person) or Ugochi dad and Adamma came (together) today.*

(E). Dialectal Difference: In Igbo language, there are occasions where dialectal expressions differ and may contradict the standard or central Igbo language meaning of that same expression even when the phonological construct is the same.

1. Ada ji aghọta ụwa – *Ada would understand what life is all about (Ngwa dialect) or Ada uses it to gain earthly understanding (standard translation).*
2. Chibụzọ <u>na-anya isi</u> -- *Chibụzọ is very pompous or Chibụzọ is sick mentally (Agụlụ dialect).*
3. E <u>were</u> ọkụ n'ụlọ Nwankwọ – *There is power outage in Nwankwọ's house or There is electricity in Nwankwọ's house (Ezeagụ dialect).*
4. Nwagbọgbọ na-esuwe ọ dị ka o ji aka nne nye – *As a young girl grows it seem it would be bigger that her mom (Nsụụka dialect) or A vomiting child that breaks out would appear to hold his/her mom's hand to give (Standard).*

Chapter 6

Solutions to Igbo linguistic Ambiguity (Idozi Mgbagwoju Anya di n'Asụsụ Igbo)

(A). Solution to Anaphoric Ambiguity: since the third person singular pronoun ("ọ") and impersonal pronouns ("a" and "e") are often the elements of linguistic ambiguity in Igbo language, it is important to apply the following method in order to bring clarity in their expression.

Introduction of descriptive word(s) or sentence in the expression: the third person singular pronoun can be used in place of a person or thing. However, by introducing a word, phrase or sentence that describe the subject, one would bring clarity to their statement or expression.

3rd person singular Igbo
She is so beautiful Ọ maka/ ọ mara ezigbo mma
He is handsome Ọ maka/ ọ mara ezigbo mma
It is so beautiful Ọ mara ezigbo mma

Notice that the pronoun "ọ" were used in place of a person as well as thing. This would pose a problem in a situation where there is no extra expression that states what or who the pronoun was referring to. For example:

English   *Igbo language*
Ada said that she is so beautiful.   Ada sị na ọ mara ezigbo mma
Ada said that he is handsome.   Ada sị na ọ mara ezigbo mma
Ada said that it is so beautiful.   Ada sị na ọ mara ezigbo mma

With preceding or extra expression the above would be:
Ada sị na ọ na-ekiri onwe ya n'enyo ụtụtụ ọbụla n'ihi na ọ mara ezigbo mma. (Igbo)

Ada said that when she looked in the mirror every morning because she is so beautiful. (English)

Ada sị na ọ lụrụ di ya n'ihi na ọ mara ezigbo mma/ ọ mara mma nwoke. (Igbo)

Ada said that she married her husband because he is a handsome man. (English)

Ada sị na ọ zụtara uwe ahụ n'ihi na ọ mara ezigbo mma. (Igbo)
Ada said that she bought that dress because it is so beautiful. (English)

Introduction of reflective personal pronouns for the known: introduce a pronoun that refers to the speaker or the person spoken to, or to a person or things whose identity is clear, usually because they have already been mentioned. For example:

First person singular Igbo
I went to market.   Ejere m ahia. ("m" refers to "I")
I asked a question.   Ajuru m ajuju. ("m" refers to "I")

3rd person plural   Igbo
They did the dishes. Asara ha efere.("ha" refers to "They")
They cooked food.   Esiri ha nri. ("ha" refers to "They")

When you take a look at the above pronouns, you would observe that the first singular and third person plural would be the same spelling and sound without the distinguishing reference pronoun.

Eliminating impersonal pronouns in third person plural statements: when you eliminate the impersonal pronoun for third person plural to make a simple straight-forward statement, your expression would be devoid of ambiguity. See example below:

They did the dishes Ha sara efere.
They cooked food   Ha siri nri.

(B) Solution to Lexicological Ambiguities: Since lexical ambiguity results from two or more words that have the same form (homonymy or homophony) or when a word has more than one meaning (polysemy), it can be disambiguated by giving little or more information in your expression. It could be by using noun instead of pronoun and/or introducing adverbial or adjectival phrase, clause or synonyms that reveal direct connection in the statement. For examples of Lexical ambiguity in Igbo language:

   1. abụ can refer to: *poem* or *armpit*

Instead use: gụọ abụ (read poem) or akpa abụ (armpit).

2. agwa can refer to: *beans* or *character*
   instead use: omume (character) or agwa nke nri (beans)

3. akwa can refer to: *bridge* or *bed*
   instead use: akwa ndina (bed) akwa ogwe (bridge)

4. anwụ can refer to: *sunshine* or *mosquito*
   instead use: anwụ nta (mosquito) or anwụ ụtụtụ, ehihe ma ọ bụ mgbede (morning, afternoon or evening sun)

5. ara can refer to: *madness* or *breast*
   instead use: ara dị n'obi (cheast breast) or ara ụbụrụ (mental illness)

6. igwe can refer to: *king* or *sky*
   instead use: elu igwe (sky) or igwe obodo (ruling king)

7. ilu can refer to: *proverb* or *bitterness*
   instead use: Ịtụ ilu (say a proverb) or Ọ dị ilu (it's bitter)

(C). *Solution to Phonological Ambiguity:* phonological ambiguities can be resolved using the tool of diacritics and tonal markings. It is recommended that written Igbo language should have both diacritics and tonal markings especially for words that are identical in spellings because they are prone to different meanings as well as interpretations..

Diacritical marks are extra symbols that are placed above or below a letter to modify the pronunciation or clarify the meaning of a word. Tone is a pitch accent that distinguishes words that are homographic. It is used in Igbo language to show the different meaning of words though they are spelt the same. Tone performs syllabic stress and semantic function in Igbo language. Tonal marking is used to show differences in words and to distinguish between declarative sentences from interrogative sentence beside the punctuation markings.

There are three distinguishing tonal marks (Akaraụdaolu) in Igbo language:

1. *Acute* (Akaraelu)   -   /
2. *Grave* (Akaraala)   -   \
3. *Macron* (Akaransụda) -   -

For examples:

1. I mara mma
a. Í mara ḿmā. (declarative) - *You are beautiful*
b. Ì mara ḿmā? (Interrogative) - *Are you beautiful*

2. I bịara ụnyaahụ.
a. Í bịara ụnyaahụ, (declarative) – *You came yesterday.*
b. Ì bịara ụnyaahụ? (interrogative) – *Did you come yesterday?*

3. O metara ya.
a. Ó metara ya. (declarative) - *He/she got it right.*
b. Ò metara ya. (interrogative) - *Did he/she got it right?*

4. Akụrụ aka n'ụzọ.
a. Ákụrụ aka n'ụzọ. (declarative) – *Someone knocked at the*

door.

b. Àkụrụ aka n'ụzọ? (interrogative) – *Did someone knock at the door?*

(D) *Solution to Structural Ambiguities*: since structural ambiguity results in a sentence with more than one grammatical structure, giving further information or using simplified grammatical phrases, clauses or sentences in your expression would help clear the vagueness and give better understanding to what is being expressed.

1. **Adaobi erighị nri ya –**
   a. Adaobi erighị nri nke ya. *Adaobi didn't eat her own food*
   b. Adaobi erighị nri nke [insert a name] *Adaobi didn't eat somebody's food.*

2. **Amaka sị na Ọ ga-abịa –**
   a. Amaka sị na ya onwe ya ga-abịa, *Amaka said that she (Amaka) would come*
   b. Amaka sị na [insert a name or description] ga-abịa *Amaka said that somebody else would come.*

3. **Gịnị butere gị ebe a? –**
   a. Gịnị mere Ị jị bia n'ebe a. *Why did you come here?*
   b. Ọ bụ ugbọ-ala butere gi n'ebe a *did you come by vehicle.*

4. **Ọ tara anụ mmadụ --**
   a. Ọ tara anụ nke enyere mmadụ *He/she ate meat that*

belongs to another person
b. Ọ tara anụ ahụ mmadụ *He/she ate human flesh.*

5. **Ndi nkuzi Igbo na-ama akwụkwọ --**
   a. Ndi nkuzi sitere n'ala Igbo na-ama akwụkwọ *Teachers of Igbo extract are brilliant*
   b. Ndi na-akuzi Igbo na-ama akwụkwọ *Teachers that teach Igbo language are brilliant.*

6. **Okọcha na-agba bọọlụ --**
   a. Okọcha bụ onye asọmumpi egwu bọọlụ *Okọcha is a football player (as career)*
   b. Okọcha na-agba bọọlụ *Okọcha is playing football (current event).*

7. **Emeka na-agụ akwụkwọ --**
   a. Emeka bụ nwata akwụkwọ *Emeka is a student*
   b. Emeka na-agụ akwụkwọ *Emeka is reading a book (current event)*

(E). Following writing rules and use of verb complement:
a. Disambiguating ambiguity by adhering to writing rules: adhering to spelling and writing rules is strictly important in bringing clarity to any non-verbal expressions. Proper punctuation as well as use of part of speech are tools for disambiguating especially between declarative and interrogative, conjunction and preposition and so on. For example:

1. **Ọlụebubu Chineke na ụlọ Ụka.**

   a. Ọlụebubu Chineke na ụlọ Ụka.

God's miracle and the Church.

b. Ọlụebubu Chineke n'ụlọ Ụka.
   God's miracle in the Church.

Notice that the simple fix to the above, was simply resolving the differences between conjunction and preposition. The first meaning uses conjunction whereas the second uses preposition as can be seen in written form. In a verbal expression there would be need to modify the above expression as in the form below for better understanding.

c. Ọlụebubu Chineke n'ime ụlọ Ụka.
   God's miracle inside the Church.

2. Ihu nwata nwaànyị ahụ dịka ihu *mma*.
a. Ihu nwata nwaànyị ahụ dịka ihu m mma –
   The girl's face is familiar.

b. Ihu nwata nwaànyị ahụ dịka ihu mma –
   The girl's face is like a machete.

Notice that the simple fix to the above, was simply by introducing relative pronoun. A relative pronoun is one which is used to refer to nouns mentioned previously, whether they are people, places, things, animals, or ideas. In a verbal expression there would be to modify the expression as in the form below for better understanding.

c. Ihu nwata nwaànyị ahụ dịka ihu mụ onwe m mma –
   The girl's face is familiar to me.

3. **Onye *mma* anọghị ya**
   a. Onye mma anọghị ya. - *The knife seller is not around.*
   b. Onye m mma anọghị ya. - *The person I know is not around.*

Notice that the simple fix to the above, was simply by introducing relative pronoun. A relative pronoun is one which is used to refer to nouns mentioned previously, whether they are people, places, things, animals, or ideas. In a verbal expression there would be to modify the expression as in the form below for better understanding.

   c. Onye na-ere mma anọghị ya. - *The knife seller is not around.*
   d. Onye ahụ m mma anọghị ya. - *The person I know is not around.*

b. Disambiguating ambiguity with the tool of verb complement: In grammar, a complement is a word, phrase, or clause that is necessary to complete the meaning of a given sentence or expression. A verb complement is a word, phrase, or clause that follows the verb to add more information. In Igbo language, verb complements are meaning specifier to Igbo verbs that can be used in two or more ways in sentence formation. For example:

1. **Eze gara.** – this is an incomplete statement because there can be up to four meanings to it as shown below:
   a. Eze gara ahịa. – *Eze went to the market.*
   b. Eze gara ụlọ akwụkwọ. – *Eze went to school.*
   c. Eze gara Ụlọ Ụka. – *Eze went to Church.*

d. Eze gara Ụlọ Ọgwu. – *Eze went to the hospital.*

2. **Ugochi gbara**. – this is an incomplete statement because there can be up to five meanings to it as shown below:
a. Ugochi gbara egwu. – *Ugochi danced.*
b. Ugoch gbara akwụkwọ. – *Ugochi wedded.*
c. Ugochi gbara ọsọ. – *Ugochi ran.*
d. Ugochi gbara asịrị. – *Ugochi gossiped.*
e. Ugochi gbara egbe.. – *Ugochi shot the gun.*

:

Chapter 7

Punctuation in Igbo Language (Akara Edemede di n'Asụsụ Igbo)

Punctuation is a special symbol used in writing to separate phrases, sentences and their elements and to clarify their meaning. They are also used to show that a sentence is a question, exclamation and so on. Examples of punctuations are full-stop/period, comma, question marks, parentheses, etc.

1. Full-stop (Kpom)
This type of punctuation is used at the end of a sentence or an abbreviation; a period. The punctuation mark or symbol for full-stop (kpom) is (.).
Examples:

English
Mary went to market.
Brian is my sibling.

Igbo
Mary jere ahia.
Brian bu nwanne m.

2. Comma (Rikom)

This type of punctuation is used to indicate a pause between parts of a sentence. It is also used to separate items in a list and to mark the place of a thousand, and so on in a large numeral. The punctuation mark or symbol for comma (Rikom) is (,).

For example:

English	Igbo
Mary bought yam, bean and corn.	Mary zutara ji, agwa na oka.
Eze has school bag, book and pen.	Eze nwere akpa akwụkwọ, akwụkwọ na mkpịsị odide.

3. Question Marks (Akara ajuju)

This type of punctuation is used in a sentence to express doubt or uncertainty about something, or to indicate a question. The punctuation mark or symbol for question mark (Akara ajuju) is (?).

For examples:

English	Igbo
How are you?	Kedụ? Kedụ ka ịmere?
Do you speak English?	Ị na-asụ Bekee?
Do you speak Igbo?	Ị na-asụ Igbo?

4. Semi-colon (Kpom Rikom)

This type of punctuation is used in a sentence to indicate a pause, typically between two main clauses, and it is more pronounced than that indicated by a comma. The punctuation mark or symbol for semi-colon (kpom) is (;).

For example:

English   **Igbo**

Peter is rich; Paul is poor.	Peter bu ogaranyi, Paul bu ogenye.

5. Colon (kpomkpom)

This type of punctuation is used to precede a list of items, a quotation, or an expansion or explanation. The punctuation mark or symbol for colon (kpom-kpom) is (:).

Examples:

English	**Igbo**
You know what to do: practice.	I ma ihe I ga-eme: tinye omumu gi n'ọrụ.
I want the following items: eraser, paper and pen	A choro m ihe ndi a: nchicha, akwukwo na mkpisi odide.

6. Apostrophe (Rikom elu)

This type of punctuation is used in a vowel dropping to indicate the omission of letter. This is especially used when "na" functions as a preposition. The punctuation mark or symbol for apostrophe (Rikom elu) is (').

Examples:

English	**Igbo**
I love you.	A hụrụ m gi n'anya.
He is at home.	Ọ nọ n'ụlọ.

7. Hyphen (Akara uhie)

This type of punctuation is used in auxiliary verb, to join words to indicate that they have a combined meaning or are linked in the grammar of a sentence. It is also used to indicate the division of a word at the end of a line, or to indicate a missing or implied element. The punctuation mark or symbol for hyphen (Akara-uhie) is (-).

Examples:

English
He will pay for everything.
Say it to me in Igbo.

Igbo
Ọ ga-akwụ ụgwọ ihe nile.
Gwa m ya na-asusu Igbo.

8. Quotation Marks (Rikom Ngwu)

This type of punctuation is used either to mark the beginning and the end of a title or quoted passage, or to indicate that the word or phrase is regarded as slang or jargon, or is being discussed rather than used within a sentence. The punctuation mark or symbol for quotation mark (Rikom Ngwu) is (' ') or (" ").

Examples:

English
"I'm very tired," she said.
"I work in Italy," said Ben.

Igbo
O siri, "Ike guru m."
Ben siri, "A na m aru—oru na obodo (mba) Italy."

9. Parentheses (Akara Nkudo)

This type of punctuation is a pair of brackets used to mark off a parenthetical word or phrase. It is also used to add extra information in a sentence. The punctuation mark or symbol for parentheses (Akara Nkudo) is ( ).

Examples:

English
Yes (all is OK).

Igbo
Ee (O di mma).

What are you called?	Gini ka anakpo g?i (aha eji mara gi).

10. Exclamation Mark (Akara Mkpu)
This type of punctuation is used with a word or phrase to indicate strong feelings (such as shock, surprise, anger or raised voice), or show emphasis, and often marks the end of the sentence. The punctuation mark or symbol for Exclamation mark (Akara mkpu) is (!).
Examples:

English	**Igbo**
Watch out!	Lee anya!
Go away!	Puo ebe a!
Leave me alone!	Hapu m aka!
Help!	Nyere m aka!
Fire!	Ọkụ!
Stop!	Kwụsi!
Call the police!	Kpoo ndi uwe ojii!

11. Slash (Akara oke)
Slash is also known as forward slash, slant, oblique dash or diagonal and is used to separate letters, numbers or words. It is also used to indicate "or". The punctuation mark or symbol for slash (Akara oke) is (/).
Examples:

English	**Igbo**
I'm good/fine.	a di m mm/O di mma.
Go straight.	gaba n'iru/ogologo.
Do you speak English/Igbo?	Ị na-asụ bekee/Igbo?

12. Ellipsis (Nsepụokwu)

This is a mark consisting of three dots (dot-dot-dot), that is used to indicate an intentional omission of a word, sentence, or whole section from a text without altering its original meaning. The punctuation mark or symbol for Ellipsis (Nsepụokwu) is (…).
Examples:

English   **Igbo**
My name is…   Aham bu …
I'm from…   Esi m na …

Part Two:

Phonology & Phonetics (Ọdịdị ụdaasụsụ na Amụmàmụ Ụdaasụsụ)

Chapter 8
Phonetics & Phonology in Igbo language:

Phonology (Ọdịdị ụdaasụsụ) is the branch of linguistics that identifies and analyzes how languages or dialects systematically organize their sounds. Phonology is the study of linguistic sound systems. Whereas Phonetics is the study of physical properties of human's speech sounds. Phonology is the classification of the sounds within the system of a particular language or languages.

Phonology, the study of the sound patterns in languages, can be divided into two parts, namely:
- Phonemes (vowels and consonants)
- Prosody (stress, rhythm and intonation)

Speaking Igbo is not easy for the people whose mother tongue is not Igbo. This is because it is a tonal language. Most of the words of a phonographic language can be pronounced according to their spelling. But most of the words of a tonal language follow their spelling as well as tonal marking during pronunciation.

Unlike Igbo language, many speech sounds in English have several different spellings, e.g. 'go', 'bow', 'row', 'know', 'though' etc. and many "same spellings" have different sounds, e.g. <ough>:

'though', 'cough', 'enough', 'bough', 'through', etc. Therefore, learners of English language cannot rely solely on the spelling of a word when they try to pronounce it.

Native speakers of Igbo language are not spared from this problem when they are new to reading and writing in Igbo. Igbo scholars, teachers and those who have took time to master Igbo phonetics may face the opposite problem as many like schoolchildren took a lot of time to learn to read and write in Igbo.

In Igbo language, the standard Igbo has thirty-six phonemes comprising twenty-eight consonants and eight vowels *(see chapter one for more details)*. This is why learning Igbo language appears to be difficult because it is like asking someone to learn the 44 phonemes of English language rather than starting from the 26 letters of English alphabets.

By learning Igbo alphabets, you learn the 36 Phonemes and will not have any other thing to worry about. Since Igbo language is a tonal language, Igbo words may differ only in tone. A typical example of tonal marking exist in 'akwa' which can assume the meaning of the following: ákwá *"cry"*, àkwà *"bed"*, àkwá *"egg"*, and ákwà *"cloth"*. As tone is not normally written, these all appear as ⟨akwa⟩ in printed format.

Igbo Phonetics (Amụmàmụ Ụdaasụsụ)

Phonetics is the study of human sounds. It is the study of physical properties of human's speech sounds. It is concerned with all aspects of the production, transmission, and perception of the sounds of language. There are three major branches of Igbo phonetics namely, acoustic, articulatory and audible.

(A). *Acoustic Phonetics* (Amụmàmụ Ọdịdị Ụda): is the study of the hearing characteristics of speech. It includes an analysis and description of vocal expression in terms of its physical properties, such as frequency, intensity, and duration.

Acoustic phonetics investigates time domain features such as the mean squared amplitude of a waveform, its duration, its fundamental frequency, or frequency domain features such as the frequency spectrum, or even combined spectrotemporal features and the relationship of these properties to other branches of phonetics (e.g. articulatory or auditory phonetics), and to abstract linguistic concepts such as phonemes, phrases, or utterances.

(B). *Articulatory Phonetics* (Amụmàmụ Mkpọpụta Ụda): Articulatory Phonetics is a branch of phonetics that deals with the motive processes and anatomy involved in the production of the sounds of speech. Articulatory phoneticians explain how humans produce speech sound through the interaction of different physiological structures. Generally, articulatory phonetics is concerned with the transformation of aerodynamic energy into acoustic energy. Aerodynamic energy refers to the airflow through the vocal tract. Its potential form is air pressure; its kinetic form is the actual dynamic airflow. Acoustic energy is variation in the air pressure that can be represented as sound waves, which are then perceived by the human auditory system as sound.

Respiratory sounds can be produced simply by expelling air from the lungs. However, to vary the sound quality in a way useful for speaking, two speech organs normally move towards each other to contact each other to create an obstruction that shapes the air in a particular fashion. The point of maximum obstruction is called the *place of articulation*, and the way the obstruction forms and releases is the *manner of articulation*. For example, when making a p sound, the lips come together tightly, blocking the air momentarily and causing a buildup of air pressure. The lips then release suddenly, causing a burst of sound. The place of articulation of this sound is therefore called *bilabial*, and the manner is called *stop* (also known as a *plosive*).

(C). *Auditory Phonetics* (Amụmàmụ Anụmụda): is the branch of phonetics that deals with the hearing of speech sounds and with speech perception. It involves the study of the relationships between speech stimuli and a listener's responses to such stimuli as mediated by mechanisms of the peripheral and central auditory systems, including certain areas of the brain. It is one of the three main branches of phonetics along with acoustic and articulatory phonetics, though with overlapping methods and questions.

Auditory phonetics is concerned with both segmental (mostly vowels and consonants) and prosodic (such as stress, tone, rhythm and intonation) aspects of speech. Most research in sociolinguistics and dialectology has been based on auditory analysis of data and almost all pronunciation dictionaries are based on impressionistic, auditory analysis of how words are pronounced.

Chapter 9

Principles of Phonemic Analysis (Usoro Ịkọwa mkpụrụụdasụsụ)

(A). Phoneme (Mkpụrụụdaasụsụ)

A phoneme (mkpụrụụdasụsụ) is a unit of sound that can distinguish one word from another in a particular language. It is represented by one or more grapheme. A grapheme is a letter or a number of letters that represent the sounds in our speech. So a grapheme will be the letter/ letters that represent a phoneme. English language has a complex written code and in English code a grapheme can be 1, 2, 3 or 4 letters. For example:

1 letter grapheme – c a r	(c)	and	m a t (m)
2 letter grapheme – team	(ea)	amd	sh i p (sh)
3 letter grapheme – sigh	(igh)	and	n igh t (igh)
4 letter grapheme – rough	(ough)	and	eigh t (eigh)

The complex nature can simply be seen by looking at the different ways various sounds are represented. For instance, some sounds (phonemes) can be spelled by different graphemes (spellings) e.g.:

- the sound /s/ can be spelled 's, se, ss, c, ce, se'
- the sound /k/ can be spelled 'c, k or ck, ch, cc, que'
- the sound /ee/ can be spelled 'ee, ea, ie, ei, e, e-e,
- the sound /o/ can be spelled 'o, a, au, aw, ough'

A digraph is a 2-letter grapheme e.g. 'ch' in 'chip', 'ss' in dress. A trigraph is a 3-letter grapheme (the clue is in 'tri') e.g. 'igh' in 'high' and 'que' in cheque. Igbo language has nine diagraph (ch, gb, gh, gw, kp, kw, nw, ny, sh) and do not have any trigraph in its grapheme.

In English, there are 44 phonemes, or word sounds that make up the language. They're divided into 19 consonants, 7 digraphs, 5 'r-controlled' sounds, 5 long vowels, 5 short vowels, 2 'oo' sounds, 2 diphthongs.

In Igbo language, phoneme is used to distinguish one word from another as well as their meanings. The 36 grapheme of Igbo phoneme which also represents the letters of Igbo alphabet can be shown to contain a pair of words that differs by one sound, thus *minimal pair*.

Minimal pairs (mkpịiche): are pairs of words that differ in only one phonological element, such as a phoneme, toneme or chroneme, and have distinct meanings. A minimally phonologically distinctive pair of words establishes a minimal distinctive linguistic sound, known as a *phoneme*, from among the acoustically distinguishable sounds in a language, known as the phones of the language.

A minimal distinctive sound is one which can distinguish one word from another when all other sounds are identical. These phones are said to be in *Contrastive Distribution*. To establish the phonemes of a language such MINIMAL PAIRS, two words differing in just one distinguishable sound (hence 'minimal'), must be found for all the phonemes.

If you cannot find a minimal pair, the phones are said to be in non-contrastive distribution. They may be in *Complementary Distribution* or in *Free Variation*.

The rules for minimum pairs are:

1. The words must have the same *number* of sounds.
2. The words must be *identical* in every sound except for one.
3. The sound that is different must be in the same *position* in each word.
4. The words must have different *meaning*.

The following are examples of minimum pairs of Phoneme in Igbo language. For example:

1st pair	2nd pair	Note
5. **Akụ** (wealth)	**Akị** (Nuts)	last vowel
6. **Ajị** (body hair)	**Ajọ** (bad)	last vowel
7. **Bi** (lives)	**Bụ** (is)	initial consonant
8. **Chere** (wait)	**Chebe** (protect)	middle consonant
9. **Eze** (teeth)	**Ezi** (Pig)	initial consonant
10. **Ọchị** (maggot)	**Ọcha** (white)	last vowel
11. **Ọka** (corn)	**Ọba** (barn)	middle consonant
12. **Ozi** (message)	**Ozu** (corpse)	last vowel

13. **Ukwe** (chorus)   **Ukwu** (waist)   *last vowel*
14. **Ụzọ** *(entrance)*   **Ụdọ** *(rope)*   *middle consonant*

Phoneme		Grapheme(s)		Examples	English
/b/	/tʃ/	/b/	/ch/	buru, churu	*carried, fetched*
/tʃ/	/d/	/ch/	/d/	cheta, deta	*remembered, write to*
/d/	/f/	/d/	/f/	dee, fee	*write, fly*
/g/	/ɓ~g͡b/	/g/	/gb/	gawa, gbawa	*proceed, break apart*
/gʷ/	/ɦ/	/gw/	/h/	gwa, ha	*tell, them*
/dʒ/	/tʃ/	/j/	/ch/	ije, iche	*walk, difference*
/k/	/tʃ/	/k/	/ch/	kee, chee	*what, think*
/ɓ~k͡p/	/kʷ/	/kp/	/kw/	kpee, kwee	*pray, agree*
/l/	/m/	/l/	/m/	mee, lee	*do, look*
/n/	/ŋʷ/	/n/	/ŋʷ/	anwụ, añụ	*sun, bee*
/ɲ/	/ŋ/	/ny/	/ñ/	anyụ, añụ	*alligator, bee*
/ọ/	/ụ/	/ọ/	/ụ/	ọka, ụka	*corn, church*
/p/	/ɹ/	/p/	/r/	panye, ranye	*pass down, commit*
/s/	/ʃ/	/s/	/sh/	ịsa, ịsha	*to wash, crayfish*
/j/	/z/	/j/	/z/	ije, ize,	*journey, dodge*
/z/	/l/	/z/	/l/	ụzọ, ụlọ	*way, house*

(B). Toneme

A toneme is a phonological element that uses pitch within spoken language as an indicator to the meaning words. English language is devoid of tonemes, but many African and Asian languages do have toneme. Igbo language is a tonal language, thus toneme is an abundant phonological element. A refreshing example is shown below:

Igbo		English	Pitch/Tonal Marking
óké	-	male	[high tone – high tone]
òkè	-	portion	[low tone – low tone]
òkè	-	boundary	[high tone – low tone]
òké	-	rat/mouse	[low tone – high tone]

(C). Chroneme

A chroneme is a phonological element that uses the duration of a syllable to determine the meaning of the word. Chroneme is not used in the English language, however, some European native languages use it. The two common examples are Latin and Italian languages. For example, the Italian word "vile" means "coward," while "ville" means "villas." In Igbo language, chroneme is not as predominate as toneme but it does exist as one of the phonological elements. For example:

1. asa *(epitome of beauty)*   asaa *(seven)*
2. be *(one's dwelling/home)*   bee *(cry)*
3. gbasa *(spread)*   gbasaa *(dismiss)*
4. isi *(head)*   isii *(six)*
5. mee *(do)*   mmee *(red)*
6. na *(and)*   nna *(father)*
7. ole *(how many/how much)*   olee *(where/when/how)*

Chapter 10

Classification of Phoneme (Nkèụdị Mkpụrụụdaasụsụ)

A phoneme is a unit of sound in speech. A phoneme doesn't have any inherent meaning by itself, but when you put phonemes together, they can make words. On the other hand, you can segment, or break apart, any word to recognize the sounds or phonemes in that word.

In order to know how many phonemes a word has, it's best to say the word out loud to focus on the sounds that make up the word rather than looking at the letters on paper. For example, if you say the word 'akị,' you will hear that there are three sound units, or phonemes, in that word: /a/ /k/ /ị/.

The two divisions of phonemes are: segmental and suprasegmental phonemes.

(a). Segmental Phonemes (Mkpụrụụdaasụsụ Ụdanke):
The ability to separate the sounds of a word is called "phoneme segmentation". Segment is the 'basic' units or 'simple sounds' which make up 'words'. It often corresponds to a written

alphabetic letter in Igbo language, even if sometimes spelling doesn't correspond nicely with pronunciation in some languages. The articulation of a particular phonemic 'segment' can be analyzed into its beginning, middle and end, any of which would be segments within that phoneme.

Phoneme represents the minimal units or one of a small speech sound. This unit of speech sound is known as segment. To determine the status of a phoneme, a substitution test is carried out. This is a method of substituting one segment with another segment such that it produces a different word.

It is recommended that by using a substitution test, one can determine if an expression qualifies as a phoneme. When a segment is replaced (substituted) by another segment and it produces a different word, then the status of segmented phoneme is established, for example, the phoneme of /e/ and /a/ in pest and past. Any pair of words as in the above that differs in one sound only or one segment is referred to as minimal pair.

Segmental Phonemes are small speech sounds (the minimal units) of a particular language that represent differences in meaning. Segmental phoneme consists of two aspects of sound's unit namely: the consonant phonemes and vowel phonemes. Mkpụrụ Edemede or Abidịị is the 36-letter alphabet of Igbo language. It features 28 consonants (mgbochiume) and 8 vowels (ụdaume).

(b). *Supra-segmental Phonemes (mkpụrụụdaasụsụ ụda-nsokwasị nke:* Supra-segmental phonemes (prosody) refer to a phonological property of more than one sound segment. As the unit of linguistic which operates above a single sound, it uses pitch, loudness, tempo, and rhythm in a speech to convey information about the structure and meaning of an utterance. Therefore, the supra-segmental phonemes features include: stress (ikeolu), intonation (ndebeolu/njeolu), duration (oge) and tone (ụdaolu).

Stress (ikeolu): stress is the degree of emphasis given a sound or syllable in speech, also called lexical stress or word stress. Stress pattern can help distinguish the meanings of two words or phrases that otherwise appear to be the same. It is the intensity given to a syllable of speech by special effort in utterance, resulting in relative loudness. For example:

Ọ dị mmā.
It is good. (Declarative)

Ọ dị mmā?
Is it good? (Interrogative)

Ọ dị mmā
If it is good. (Conditional)

Intonation (ndebeolu/njeolu): intonation is the melodic pattern of an utterance. It is used to convey emotions such as surprise, anger, or delight), and other differences of expressive meaning. It can also serve a grammatical function. Intonation is primarily a matter of variation in the pitch of the voice. Intonation describes how the voice rises and falls in speech.

Length/Duration (oge): is a feature of sounds that have distinctively extended length or quantity compared with other sounds.

Contour tone (ụdaolu ngwe): contour describes speech sounds which behave as single segments, but which make an internal transition from one quality, place, or manner to another. These sounds may be tones, vowels, or consonants. Many tone languages have contour tones, which move from one level to another or shift from one pitch to another over the course of the syllable or word. There are two contour tones in Igbo—the rising and the falling tones.

Tones: Igbo has three tones, high, mid, and low, which are phonemic, serving to make lexical, grammatical and syntactical distinctions. The mid-tone can only follow a high-tone and, in consequence, is absent in monosyllables. For example:

Acute	Macron	Grave
(High tone)	(Mid tone)	(Low tone)
/	-	\
Á	Ā	À

In pronunciation, tone distinguishes pitch level of a syllable. These are examples of their usage in the Igbo language:

ákwá	-	cry	[high tone – high tone]
àkwá	-	egg	[low tone – high tone]
àkwà	-	bridge/bed	[low tone – low tone]
ákwà	-	cloth	[high tone – low tone]

ísí	-	head	[high tone – high tone]
ìsì	-	blindness	[low tone – low tone]
ísì	-	smell	[high tone – low tone]
ìsí	-	to cook	[low tone – high tone]
óké	-	male	[high tone – high tone]
òkè	-	portion	[low tone – low tone]
ókè	-	boundary	[high tone – low tone]
òké	-	rat/mouse	[low tone – high tone]
ḿmā	-	good/beautiful	[high tone – mid tone]
ḿmà	-	knife	[high tone – low tone]

Igbo Consonants:

In the alphabet system, consonants are a somewhat easier concept to represent than vowels. A consonant involves some part of the tongue or lips touching or coming close to some other part of the mouth — lips, teeth, roof of the mouth in various places. The consonant system of Igbo language has major features, namely: doubly articulated consonants and labialized Velars.

Doubly articulated consonants: these are consonants with two simultaneous places of articulation – *bilabial* and *velar*. Bilabial and velar are produced in the same manner. Both of them are produced as stops. /k͡p/ and /g͡b/ are the two examples of bilabial and velar. One can pronounce these sounds, by trying to say [k] or [g], with close lips as one would for [p] or [b].

Labialized velar or labiovelar: is a velar consonant that is labialized, with a /w/-like secondary articulation. Secondary articulation occurs when the articulation of a consonant is equivalent to the combined articulations of two or three simpler consonants, at least one of which is an approximant. Maledo (2011) defines secondary articulation as the superimposition of lesser stricture upon a primary articulation. Common examples are [k^w, g^w, x^w, $ŋ^w$], which are pronounced like a [k, g, x, ŋ], with rounded lips, such as the labialized voiceless velar plosive [k^w]. The three labialized velars in Igbo language falls between voiced stop, fricative voiceless and nasals. They are /k^w/, /g^w/ and /$ŋ^w$/. To produce these sounds, one would need to try pronouncing [k], [g] or [ng] with rounded lips.

Upper case	Lower case	Phoneme	English	Igbo
B	b	/b/	bat	bia
CH	ch	/t͡ʃ/	chop	chi
D	d	/d/	dot	dee
F	f	/f/	fat	fee
G	g	/g/	go	gi
GB	gb	/g͡ɓ/	jaw	agba
GH	gh	/ɣ/	war	agha
GW	gw	/gʷ/	ling*ui*ne	gwa
H	h	/ɦ/	happy	ha
J	j	/d͡ʒ/	job	njem
K	k	/k/	key	kele
KP	kp	/k͡p/ -	left (hand)	ekpe
KW	kw	/kʷ/	q*ueen*ie	kwere
L	l	/l/	lie	Lee
M	m	/m/	me	mu
N	n	/n/	never	nne
Ṅ	ṅ	/ŋ/	song	anụ
NW	nw	/ŋʷ/	winter	nwere

NY	ny	/ɲ/	canyon	nye
P	p	/p/	pet	pụta
R	r	/ɹ/	rent	rie
S	s	/s/	sit	sara
SH	sh	/ʃ/	shop	ịsha
T	t	/t/	tell	teta
V	v	/v/	vet	vum
W	w	/w/	wet	were
Y	y	/j/	yet	ya
Z	z	/z/	zag	zaa

Igbo Vowels:

The sound inventory of Standard Igbo consists of eight vowels. Igbo vowels are divided into two major mutual exclusive groups. Group "aịọụ" are referred to as light vowels, and group "a" while group eiou are known as heavy vowels and "e" group. The heavy vowels "eiou" occur with advanced tongue root (+ATR) while the light vowels "aịọụ" occur with retracted tongue root (-ATR).

The vowel segments in +ATR group /eiou/ harmonize among themselves and those in the –ATR class /aịọụ/ harmonize among themselves during simple word formation (especially in the formation of simple nouns).

The vowel segments in +ATR group /eiou/ in a harmonized form:

àbàdà - *(abada cloth)*
áhíhíá - (*grasses*)
Ákpúkpá - (*scabies*)
Ákwúkwó - *(book)*
Ákwà - (*egg*)

ábúzù - *(cricket)*
àkpà - *(bag)*
átúrú - (sheep)
Àzù - (*fish*)
Àzúzú - (*catarrh*)

Ánú - (*meat*)
Gòté - (*buy*)
Ókpùrùkpù - (*lump*)
Ónwú - (*death*)
Úlò - (*house*)

bịá - (*come*)
Ọkpụkpụ - (*bone*)
Òkúkò - (*chicken/fowl*)
Ózúzú (*training*)

The vowel segments in -ATR group /eiou/ in a harmonized form:

égō - (*money*)
élū - (*top, up*)
éwú - (*goat*)
ézē - (*teeth*)
Ókpórókō - (*stock fish*)
Ólùlù - (*pit*)
Ósísí - (*tree/stick*).

ègwúsí - (*melon*)
éríméri - (*food*)
ézè - (*king*)
Ógólógó - (*long, tall*)
ókwú - (*speech/talk*)
Óríri - (*feast*)

Igbo Vowel Harmony in Verb form:

bàtáwá	come in	bèté	cut off
bùtá (gbutu e)	uproot	fèé	fly
gaa	go	gbàwá	runaway
gbúbìté	cut out	gbúpù	cut out
gbùté	cut out	jèé	go
kpòtéwé	collect	mèé	do
nyèwé	give	nyùá	excrete
ríé	eat	rìwé	eat on
sàcháá	wash	sìé	cook
tútúà	pick up	zùtá	buy

There are areas where vowel harmony rules in Igbo language are violated. As a result, there are two main exceptions from Vowel

Harmony Rules in Igbo Language. They are: Loan or Borrowed Words and compound words.

A. Vowel harmony violation via borrowed words, Examples:

Akpati - *box* (Yoruba)   Agidi - *Corn food* (Yoruba)
Àsháwó – *prostitute* (Yoruba) Sájìn - *sergeant* (English)
Sójà - *soldier* (English)   ịchàfú - *chiffon* (French)
Osikápá- *chinkafa* (Hausa)   Òbàsì - (abasi God) (Efik)

The above words through socioeconomic interaction were either borrowed or coined from words obtained in different languages and introduced into Igbo language vocabularies.

B. Examples of vowel harmony violation via Compound Words or Compounding: Compound words or compounding are words which are formed by combining two simple words to form one word in Igbo languages. These are words formed through morphological indigenous resources. Words from different vowel classes can combine to form compound words and such words can never harmonize. Let us examine the formation of the following proper nouns in Igbo language and with their violation of vowel harmony rules.

a. Àdá + Òbì Àdáóbì (First daughter)
b. Àdá + Ézè Àdáèzè (Princess)
c. Ífé + Ómá Íféómá (Goodies/Good thing)
d. Ísì + àkú Ísíàkú (head of wealth)
e. Èké + ḿmā Èkéḿmā (good market day)

Pitch-Accent in Igbo Pitch accent manifests in two basic ways in Igbo (a) Lexically (b) phrasal/sentential form. The tonal phenomenon in Igbo that lends credence to the existence of pitch accent in Igbo language is the alternation of pitch, as it were, among grammatical structures.

For instance, for the declarative sentence the verb root must bear the low tone irrespective of their inherent tones. As can be seen in the future particle using the prefix 'ga'--'ga' must bear a low tone while the verb root to which it is prefixed retains its inherent tone.

In future tense:

    a. me'   gà-èmé   'will do'
    b. pú   gà-èpú   'will germinate'
    c. wè   gà-éwè   'will take'
    d. zà   gà-ázà   'will sweep'
    e. zú   gà-àzú   'will buy'

In past tense:

    a. Ó biàrà zúó, ríé, núó, láá.
    He/she came bought, ate, drank (and) left.

    b. Yáá pùó, dàá, wùó, bàá ń'úlo.
    He/she went out, fell, jumped (and) entered the house.

In the serialization of Igbo verbs there is also a fixed pitch pattern. As can be seen in the following examples; when the inherent tone on the verb root is high, its pitch is retained and followed by a high toned suffix. On the other hand, when the inherent tone is low, it is followed by a high toned suffix. For example:

In words:

a. mé	mèé	*'to do'*
b. pú	pùrù	*'germinated'*
c. wè	wèré	*'take'*
d. zà	zàá	*'sweep'*
e. zụ	zùó	*'buy'*

In syllable/sentence:

a. mé	méghì	*'did not do'*
b. pú	púghì	*'did not germinate*
c. wè	wéghì	*'did not take'*
d. zá	zághì	*'did not sweep'*
e. zú	zúghì	*'did not buy'*

The above examples show that in each example the pitch makes a syllable prominent. It could be high or low but it is predictable based on the syntactic structure of the utterance.

Chapter 11

The organ of speech (Njiakpọ Okwu)

An organ is a part of an organism that is typically self-contained and has a specific vital function. Speech organs also known as vocal organs are the various organs which are involved in the production of speech sounds. The study of speech organs helps us to determine the role of each organ in the production of speech sounds. The organs of speech can be divided into three systems:

1. The respiratory system
2. The phonatory system
3. The articulatory system

The respiratory system (Ọwa Nkuume): this comprises of the lungs, the muscles of the chest and the windpipe. There are three air-stream mechanisms of the respiratory system. They are: Pulmonic (Ingressive & Egressive), Glottalic (Pharyngeal) and Velaric (Oral air-stream mechanism).

1. *Pulmonic airstream* (Akpọmụda Nsinangụ): Most speech sounds are produced by pushing lung air out of the body through

the mouth and sometimes also through the nose. Since lung air is used, these sounds are called pulmonic sounds; since the air is pushed out, they are called egressive.

Pulmonic ingressive describes ingressive sounds in which the airstream is created by the lungs. These are generally considered paralinguistic. They may be found as phonemes, words, and entire phrases on all continents and in genetically-unrelated languages, most frequently in sounds for agreement and back channeling.

2, *Glottalic airstream mechanism* (Akpọmụda Nsineeko) involves the movement of pharynx air by the action of the glottis. An upward movement of the closed glottis will move the air out of the mouth; a downward movement of the closed glottis will cause air to be sucked into the mouth.

3. *Velaric airstream mechanism* (Akpọmụda Nsinaakpo) involves the movement of mouth air by action of the tongue. There is a velar closure formed by raising the back of the tongue when using the velaric airstream mechanism. The movement of lung air by the respiratory muscles. Most sounds are produced with a pulmonic airstream (Akpọmụda Nsinàngù) mechanism.

The phonatory system: Comprises the larynx. The larnyx is situated at the top of the wind pipe and the air from the lungs. The air from the lungs has to pass through the wind pipe and the larynx. In the larynx there is a lip-like structure called the vocal cords or vocal folds—but "folds" is a more accurate description of what they're actually like.

The larynx or voice box is the basis for all the sounds we produce. It modified the airflow to produce different frequencies of sound. By changing the shape of the vocal tract and airflow, we are able to produce all the phonemes of spoken language.

There are two basic categories of sound that can be classified in terms of the way in which the flow of air through the vocal tract is modified. Phonemes that are produced without any obstruction to the flow of air are called vowels. Phonemes that are produced with some kind of modification to the airflow are called consonants. Of course, nature is not as clear-cut as all that and we do make some sounds that are somewhere in between these two categories. These are called semivowels and are usually classified alongside consonants as they behave similar to them.

The opening between the vocal folds (when it exists) is called the **glottis**. Sounds produced with wide-open glottis are called voiceless sounds (Udaogbi), e.g: peel, ten, thin, etc. Sounds produced when the vocal cords vibrate are called voiced sounds (ụdamputa), eg: bead, judge, zoo, etc.

The articulatory system: this comprises of the nose, the teeth, the tongue, the roof of the mouth and the lips. The roof of the mouth comprises the teeth-ridge, the hard palate, the soft palate and the uvula.

Since the production of consonants requires modification to the airflow, unlike vowels, an obstruction is produced by bringing some parts of the vocal tract into contact. These places of contact are known as places of articulation. There are a number of places of articulation for the lips, teeth, and tongue. Sometimes the articulators touch each other as in the case of the two lips coming together to produce [b]. At other times, two articulators come into contact as when the lower lip folds back into the upper teeth to produce [f]. The tongue can touch different parts of the vocal tract to produce a variety of consonants by touching the teeth, the alveolar ridge, hard palate or soft palate (or velum).

The Tongue (Ire): The tongue is the most important articulator of speech. This muscle is extremely strong, as it must move food around in our mouths as we chew. The tongue is a large muscular structure that nearly fills the oral cavity. The tongue is not one large muscle as some might suppose but consists of several muscles grouped as intrinsic and extrinsic tongue muscles. The tongue is able to produce incredibly fine and complex movements, by either directing the breath stream during consonant production or elevating and lowering to form a resonance vessel for vowel sounds.

In Igbo speech sound, the tongue can be divided into the front (ihu ire); which lies underneath the hard palate when the tongue is at rest, the center (ùgbò ire); which is partly beneath the hard palate and partly beneath the soft palate; and the back (àzụ ire); which is beneath the soft palate; and the root, which is opposite the back wall of the pharynx. The tip is the extreme end of the tongue. The blade lies opposite to the alveolar ridge. The front lies opposite to the hard palate. And the back lies opposite to the *soft palate*/velum (akpo ime).

The tongue is responsible for the production of many speech sounds since it can move very fast to different places and is also capable of assuming different shapes. The shape and the position of the tongue are crucial for the production of vowel sounds. Thus when we describe the vowel sounds in the context of the function of the tongue, we generally consider the following criteria:

Tongue Height: this is concerned with the vertical distance between the upper surface of the tongue and the *hard palate* (akpọime). With this condition, vowels can be described as close and open.

Tongue Frontness / Backness: this is concerned with the part of the tongue between the front and the back, which is raised high. From this point of view, the vowel sounds can be classified as front vowels and back vowels. By changing the shape of the tongue we can produce vowels in which a different part of the tongue is the highest point. That means a vowel having the back of the tongue as the highest point is a back vowel, whereas the one having the front of the tongue as the highest point is called a front vowel.

For speech sound to resonate effectively, the less tongue root tension (i.e. tension in the *extrinsic* muscles of the tongue), the better. For speech you want to relax the tongue up and forward, the opposite of swallowing.

The lips (Egbugbere Ọnụ): The lips play a role in changing the resonance of different speech sounds. Human beings are **Bilabial** (two lips)—lower lip and upper lip. A bilabial sound is produced by using both lips pressed together. By altering the shape of our lips we can form different speech sounds. For instance, for plosive sounds such as /p/ and /b/ the lips are compressed and then opened to produce a rapid, explosive release of the breath stream.

Also, the lips and *teeth* (eze) can interact to produce speech sound. This is known as Labiodental (lips and teeth) articulation. A labiodental sound is produced by placing the upper teeth on the lower lip. There are two common labiodental sounds: [f] voiceless (Udaogbi) and [v] voiced.

The lungs (Ngụ): The lungs are two elastic sacs in the chest that draw in air (mainly to oxygenate the blood). To initiate speech, they push air back up through the windpipe towards the voice box. When air from the lungs reaches the larynx (through *respiration system* (Ọwa Nkuume)), the vocal folds may be held open to allow the air to pass through or may vibrate to make a sound (phonation). The airflow from the lungs is then shaped by the articulators in the mouth and nose (articulation).

The Uvular (Àshà/Nkọlọ): this is the small fleshy mass that hangs from the back of the velum; at the entrance to the throat. Uvular is a place of articulation where the passive articulator is the uvula. A uvular can also be a specific consonant made at that place of articulation often with the back of the tongue against or near the uvula, that is, further back in the mouth than velar consonants.

The teeth (Eze): Human teeth are crucial in the making of speech sound. Speech sounds are complex and they are produced using our teeth, lips, tongue and vocal cords. Some sounds such as vowels are formed without using teeth or lips, but many sounds rely solely on the contact between our lips and teeth or our tongue and our teeth. Human teeth help form words by controlling airflow out of the mouth. Also, our tongue strikes our teeth or the roof of our mouth as some sounds are made.

Missing molars and premolars won't affect your speech too much, but if you have any front teeth missing, you may struggle to pronounce certain sounds. If a child has lost their front teeth, then we would expect his speech sound to 'sound a little different'. In general, the loss of teeth leads to an articulation difference. Teeth are needed for a variety of sounds we use in the Igbo language, like the **"sh"** sound in **"Ịsha,"** **the "f"** in **"Ifeọma,"** the **"s"** in **"Sìrì,"** and the "ch" in **"Chibụeze."**

Chapter 12

Place of Articulation (Ebe Mkpọpụta Ụda)

As earlier explained, the standard Igbo alphabet (I*Mkpụrụ Edemede Igbo*), otherwise known as the Abịidịị Igbo, is made up of 36 letters, which includes only a 23-letter set of the ISO basic Latin alphabet with the exemption of C, Q, and X, which are not part of Abidịị Igbo.

The 36-letter alphabet (*Mkpụrụ Edemede* or *Abidịị*) has 28 consonants (*mgbochiume*) and 8 vowels (*ụdaume*). Igbo alphabet uses the diacritics (a dot, an overline, overscore, or overbar above) on the letter Ṅ or Ñ, and the dot below three of the eight vowels; Ị, Ọ and Ụ.

A	B	Ch	D	E	F	G	Gb	Gh
Gw	H	I	Ị	J	K	Kp	Kw	L
M	N	Nw	Ny	Ṅ	O	Ọ	P	R
Ṣ	Sh	T	U	Ụ	V	W	Y	Z

The 36-letter alphabet (*Mkpụrụ Edemede* or *Abidịị*) has the grapheme of Igbo Phoneme as shown below:

a	b	t͡ʃ	d	e	f	g	g͡b	ɣ
gʷ	ɦ	i	ị	d͡ʒ	k	k͡p	kʷ	l
m	n	ŋ	ŋʷ	ɲ	o	ọ	p	ɹ
s	ʃ	t	u	ụ	v	w	j	z

As already explained, a phoneme (mkpụrụụdasụsụ) is a unit of sound that can distinguish one word from another in a particular language. It is represented by one or more grapheme. A grapheme is a letter or a number of letters that represent the sounds in our speech. So a grapheme will be the letter/ letters that represent a phoneme.

Having given a brief background, let us look at the subject of speech articulation. The location at which two speech organs approach or come together to produce a speech sound; as in the contact of the tongue and the teeth to form a dental sound; is called *the place of articulation*. It is also called point of articulation.

The Articulators: The 'articulators' are the instruments (e.g. your lips, lungs, tongue, etc.) used to make a sound. The locations on the mouth, where the articulators are placed, may also refer to as the 'places of articulation'. Example: The two lips (the articulators) meet to form the bilabial sounds of /b/ and /p/. When making a p sound, the lips come together tightly, blocking the air momentarily and causing a buildup of air pressure. The lips then release suddenly, causing a burst of sound. The articulator are divided into two, namely:
1. Active articulator (Njiakpọike)
2. Passive articulator (Njiakpọjụụ).

During articulation, there is constriction between both articulators. The parts that makes up the *active articulators* are the lower lip and the tongue, while the *passive articulators* are the upper lip, the upper teeth, the roof of the mouth, and the rear wall.

Active articulator: This is part of the vocal tract which moves towards the *passive articulator* to form a constriction during the articulation of a sound. It does all or most of the movement during sound articulation. During the speech sound's production, the active articulator moves towards the passive articulator and causes complete or partial obstruction of the flow of air in the vocal tract. This part includes, lips (labial), tongue tip (apical), tongue blade (laminal), tongue body (dorsal) and tongue root (radical).

Passive articulator: This is part of the vocal tract that are normally fixed and are the parts with which the active articulator makes contact with to form a constriction during the articulation of a sound. It is the part of the vocal tract that is more stationary. This part includes, lips (labial), upper teeth (dental), alveolar ridge (alveolar), postalveolar region (postalveolar), hard palate (palatal), soft palate (velar), uvula (uvular) and pharyngeal wall (pharyngeal).

During speech sound articulation, the above listed passive articulators usually pair with the moving part of the vocal tract (active articulator) in the following manners:

Passive articulator	*Active articulator(s)*
Alveolar ridge	tongue tip, tongue blade
Hard palate	tongue body (sometimes tongue tip)
Lip	the other lip

Pharyngeal wall	tongue root
Postalveolar region	tongue blade, tongue tip
Soft palate	tongue body
Upper teeth	lower lip, tongue blade, tongue tip
Uvula	tongue body

At each place of articulation, there is a constriction between an active articulator and a passive articulator. The degree of the constriction is known as Constriction degree. The three most common degrees of constriction are stop, fricative, and approximant.

The five major human body's organs of speech that constitute place of articulation in Igbo phonetics are lips (egbubere Ọnụ), tongue (ire), teeth (eze), Soft Palate (Akpo ime), Hard Palate (Akpo ihu) and Teeth Alveolar/ridge (anyụrụ).

Structure of Place of Articulation diagram
(Ihe osise njiakpọ okwu)

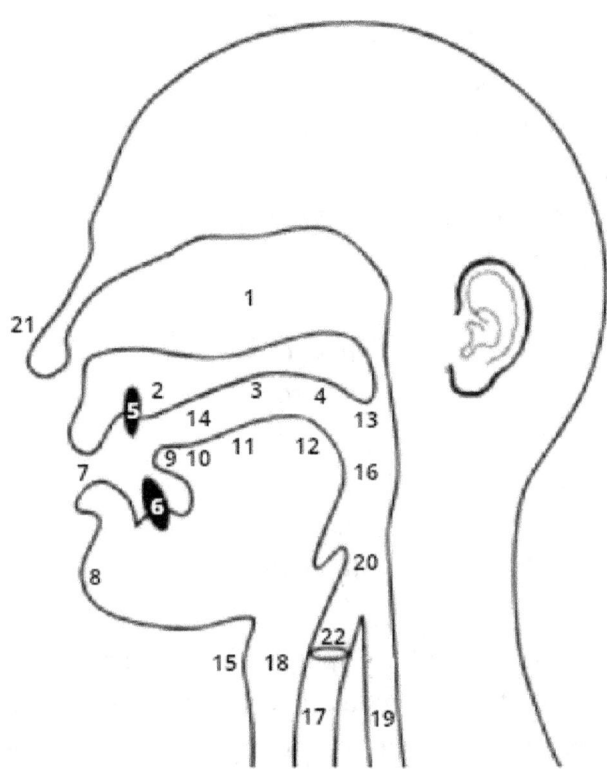

List of the parts shown (Aha na mkpọpụta ihe osise)

	English	**Igbo**
1.	*Nasal cavity*	Uju imi
2.	*Alveolar ridge*	Anyụrụ
3.	*Hard palate*	Akpo ihu
4.	*Velum/soft palate*	Akpo ime
5.	*Upper Teeth*	Eze elu
6.	*Lower teeth*	Eze ala
7.	*Lips*	Egbugbere Ọnụ
8.	*Jaw*	Agba

9.	*Tongue tip*	Ọnụ ire
10.	*Front of tongue*	Ihu ire
11.	*Blade of tongue*	Ugbo ire
12.	*Back of Tongue*	Azụ ire
13.	*Uvula*	Ụvụla
14.	*Oral/Buccal Cavity*	Uju Ọnụ
15.	*Adam's apple*	Eko akpịrị
16.	*Pharynx*	Nkọlọ
17.	*Trachea/Wind pipe*	Opi akpịrị
18.	*Larynx*	Ogworo
19.	*Esophagus*	Ọwa nri
20.	*Epiglottis*	Asha
21.	*Nose*	Imi
22.	*Vocal cord*	Mkpọuda

Larynx comprises: Epiglottis, Supraglottis, Vocal cord, Glottis and Subglottis. Vocal folds are a two thick flaps of muscle rather like a pair of lips. **Pharynx** is a tube which begins just above the larynx. **Soft palate/velum** allows air to pass through the nose and through the mouth. Hard palate is the roof of the mouth. **Alveolar ridge** is between the top front teeth and the hard palate. The **tongue** has the capacity to move into different places and form different shapes. The **tongue root** (Ukwu ire) is the part at the far back and bottom of the tongue, forming the front wall of the pharynx. **Nasal cavity** is a large air filled space above and behind the nose in the middle of the face. **Oral cavity** is the part of the mouth behind the gums and teeth that is bounded above by the hard and soft palates and below by the tongue. Lips are the two soft edges at the opening to the mouth.

Place of Vowel Articulation (Ebe Mkpoputa Udaume)

Igbo language oral vowel phonemes are made up of eight vowels. The letters that make up the Igbo vowels are:

a   e   i   o   u   ị   ọ   ụ

The graphemes that made up the Igbo vowels are:

a   e   i   o   u   ɪ   ɔ   ʊ

The vowels articulation chart is a way of showing the mouth and different positions of the tongue when a vowel sound is produced. The chart below shows the grapheme of Igbo vowels.

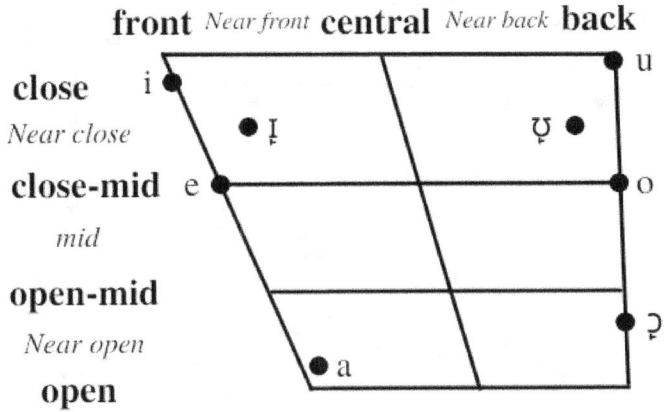

The vowels articulation transcription chart in English is shown below:

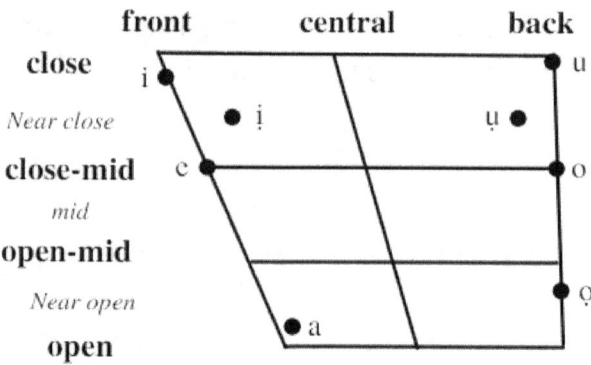

The vowels articulation transcription chart in Igbo is shown below:

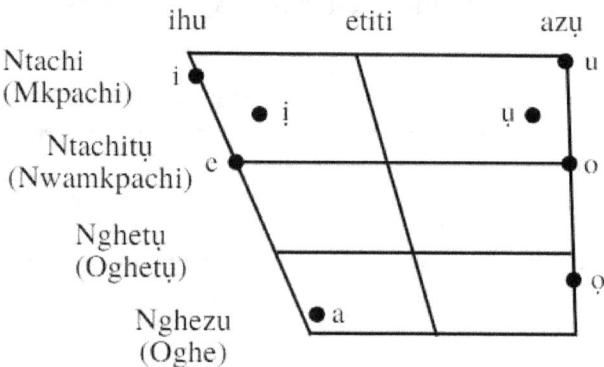

From the above vowel articulation chart, the following are the breakdown of the Igbo vowel articulation.

A. Front Vowels (Ụdaume ihu)
Front vowels located at the left-hand-side of the chart refer to vowels articulated towards the front of the mouth. To produce these vowels, the tongue rolls forward towards the front position of the mouth. This can either refer to vowels that are more front than central or, more rarely, only to fully front vowels, i.e. the ones that

are articulated as far forward as possible in the mouth. For example:

Close (Ntachi/Mkpachi)	*pronounces*	/i/.
Near Close-mid (Ntachitụ/Nwamkpachi)	*pronounces*	/ị/.
Near Open (Nghetụ/Oghetụ)	*pronounces*	/e/.
Open (Nghezu/Oghe)	*pronounces*	/a/.

B. Back Vowels (Ụdaume Azụ)
Back vowels refer to vowels that are articulated as back as possible in the mouth. To produce back vowel, the tongue tends to pull back. For example:

Close (Ntachi/Mkpachi)	*pronounces*	/u/.
Close-mid (Ntachitụ/Nwamkpachi)	*pronounces*	/ụ/.
Open-mid (Nghetụ/Oghetụ)	*pronounces*	/o/.
Open (Nghezu/Oghe)	*pronounces*	/ọ/.

C. Close and Close-mid Vowels
(Ụdaume Ntachi/Mkpachi na Ntachitụ/Nwamkpachi)
Close vowel is a class of vowel sounds that is produced, during articulation, when the tongue is positioned as close as possible to the roof of the mouth as it can be without creating a constriction. A constriction would produce a sound that would be classified as a consonant. The two vowels involved are: /i/ and /u/.

A close-mid vowel (also mid-close vowel, high-mid vowel, mid-high vowel or half-close vowel) is any in a class of vowel sound produced when the tongue is positioned one third of the way from a close vowel to an open vowel. The two vowels involved are: /ị/ and /ụ/.

Examples of tabular representation:

Articulation	*Front (Ihu)*	*Back (Azụ)*
Close (Ntachi/Mkpachi)	/i/	/u/
Close-mid (Ntachitụ/Nwamkpachi)	/ị/	/ụ/

D. Near Open and Open Vowels (Nghetụ (Oghetụ) na Nghezu (Oghe))

Open-mid vowel is a class of vowel sounds that is produced, during articulation, when the tongue is positioned between an open vowel (a low vowel) and a near open vowel. For example: /a/ and /ọ/. Open vowels are vowels that are more open than a mid-vowel. Examples of open vowels are:/a/ and /ọ/

Examples:

Articulation	*Front (Ihu)*	*Back (Azụ)*
Near open (Nghetụ/Oghetụ)	/e/	/o/
Open (Nghezu/Oghe)	/a/	/ọ/

Place of consonants articulation (Ebe Mkpoputa Mgbochiume).

The consonant sounds are produced with partial or total obstruction to the flow of air coming through the lungs to the mouth. In the production of the consonant sounds, the opening and close of the glottis is key. When the glottis (the opening between the vocal cords) is wide open, there is no vibration in the voice box and this results in the production of voiceless consonant sounds (Udaogbi Mgbochiume). When the glottis is narrow (almost closed), there is a vibration in the voice box therefore the sounds being produced are voiced consonant sounds (ụdamputa Mgbochiume).

Consonants are speech sound that is characterized by an articulation with a closure or narrowing of the vocal tract such that a complete or partial blockage of the flow of air is produced. Consonants are usually classified according to *place of articulation* (the location of the stricture made in the vocal tract, such as dental, bilabial, or velar), *the manner of articulation* (the way in which the obstruction of the airflow is accomplished, as in stops, fricatives, approximants, trills, taps, and laterals), and *the presence or absence of voicing, nasalization, aspiration, or other phonation.*

There are 28 letters as well as grapheme of Igbo consonants. The letter are as follows:

b	ch	d	f	g	gb	gh
gw	h	j	k	kp	kw	l
m	n	nw	ny	ṅ	p	r
s	sh	t	v	w	y	z

The grapheme of Igbo consonants are as follows:

b	t͡ʃ	d	f	g	g͡ɓ	ɣ
gʷ	ɦ	d͡ʒ	k	k͡p	kʷ	l
m	n	ŋ	ŋʷ	ɲ	p	ɹ
s	ʃ	t	v	w	j	z

Consonants Phoneme's chart

Manner of Articulation	VOICING	Bilabial	Labiodental	Alveolar	Palatoalveolar	Velar Plain	Velar Labial	Labial Velar	Glottal
STOP	Voiced	b		d		g	gʷ	g͡b	
STOP	Voiceless	p		t		k	kʷ	k͡p	
AFFRICATE	Voiceless				tʃ				
AFFRICATE	Voiced				dʒ				
FRICATIVE	Voiceless		f	s	ʃ				h
FRICATIVE	Voiced		v	z		ɣ			
GLIDE	Voiced					j		w	
NASAL	Voiced	m		n	ɲ	ŋ	ŋʷ		
RHOTIC	Voiced			ɾ					
LATERAL	Voiced			l					

THE PLACE OF ARTICULATION

Consonants Alphabet's chart

Manner of Articulation		VOICING	THE PLACE OF ARTICULATION								
			Bilabial	Labiodental	Alveolar	Palatoalveolar	Velar		Labial Velar	Glottal
							Plain	Labial		
STOP		Voiced	b		d		g	gw	gb	
		Voiceless	p		t		k	kw	kp	
AFFRICATE		Voiceless				ch				
		Voiced				j				
FRICATIVE		Voiceless		f	s	sh				
		Voiced		v	z		gh			h
GLIDE		Voiced					y		w	
NASAL		Voiced	m		n	ny	ṅ	nw		
RHOTIC		Voiced			r					
LATERAL		Voiced			l					

Chaatị Mkpọpụta Ụda Mgbochiume

Mkpụrụ Ụda Mgbochiume

Usoro Mkpoputa Mgbochiume	Ebe Mkpoputa	Egbugbere Ọnụ abụọ	Egbugbere na Eze	Egbugbere na Akpo	Akpo ihu	Akpo ime	Anyụrụ na Akpo	Akpiri (Eko)
ỤDAIKE	Kendakpu			gw kw				
ỤDAIKE	Keọkpọrọ (Kendaputa)	p b				k g	t d	
ỤDAIKE	Kemkponegbugbere	gb kp						
ỤDARỊỊ	Keọkpọrọ						r	
ỤDAYỊỊ	keegbugberenaakpo	w			y			
ỤDAIMI	Keọkpọrọ	m			ny	ṅ	n	
ỤDAIMI	Kemkponeegbugbere					nw		
ỤDALỊỊ	Keanyụrụnaakpo						l	
ỤDACHỊỊ	Kemkponaakpo				ch j			
ỤDASHỊỊ	Keọkpọrọ		f v		sh	gh	s z	h

Chapter 13

Transcription of Igbo Phonemes (Ndepụtagharị Mkpụrụụdaasụsụ Igbo)

Phonetic transcription (also known as phonetic script or phonetic notation) is the visual representation of speech sounds (or phones) by means of symbols. The most common type of phonetic transcription uses a phonetic alphabet, such as the International Phonetic Alphabet (IPA).

IPA in Igbo Phonetics
International Phonetic Alphabet (IPA) was developed in the XIX century but is presently used for the modern language. The International Phonetic Alphabet is a system of symbols representing each sound used in the Igbo language. Linguists transcribe words in this alphabet for their research. Dictionaries use IPA to present the correct pronunciation of words. The two broad categories of International Phonetic Alphabet (IPA) are vowels and consonants.

IPA Chart and its usage

The IPA chart is a unique classification of sounds according to different aspects. There are 107 phonetic symbols and 52 diacritics in this phonemic transcription chart. Each of them represents its place in the mouth or throat. The manner in which sounds are pronounced depends on how lips, tongue, teeth and the palate work to produce them.

The IPA phonemes of Igbo language is used in transcription from Alphabet to Grapheme. The following is the representation of both with accompanying examples.

Upper case	Lower case	IPA phonemes	Examples
A	a	a	*aka, akụ*
B	b	b	*bịa, buru*
CH	ch	t͡ʃ	*chidi, chim*
D	d	d	*duru, dim*
E	e	e	*eze, ede*
F	f	f	*fere, fechi*
G	g	g	*gịnị, gụrụ*
GB	gb	g͡ɓ	*gbara, gburu*
GH	gh	ɣ	*ghe, ghọta*
GW	gw	gʷ	*gwa, gwọọ*
H	h	ɦ	*hapụ, họrọ*
I	i	i	*ite, iche*
Ị	ị	ɪ	*ịgba, ịchaka*
J	j	d͡ʒ	*jere, ji*
K	k	k	*kele, kama*
KP	kp	k͡p	*kpakpando*
KW	kw	kʷ	*kwuru, kwere*
L	l	l	*lee, leta*

152

M	m	m	mere, mma
N	n	n	nna, nwa
Ṅ	ṅ	ŋ	aṅụ, ọṅụ
NW	nw	ŋʷ	enwe, ọnwa
NY	ny	ɲ	nye, enyo
O	o	o	osisi, ose
Ọ	ọ	ɔ	ọsa, ọka
P	p	p	pọọpọ, pụta
R	r	ɹ	riri, rechara
S	s	s	siri, sere
SH	sh	ʃ	ịsha, ịchafụ
T	t	t	teta, taa
U	u	u	uwe, ume
Ụ	ụ	ʊ	ụwa, ụkwụ
V	v	v	mvọ isi
W	w	w	weta, wwere
Y	y	j	ya, nyọ
Z	z	z	zụta, azịza

Application of the Transcription and usage

The following examples show how Igbo words are transcribed in order to allow easy pronunciation from anyone who knows IPA symbols or graphemes without any need of assistance.

Word	**Mkpụrụokwu**	***Transceiption***
Camel	Ịnyịya ibu	/ɪɲja ibu/
Cat	Nwamba/Nwologbo	/ŋʷamba/ or /ŋʷolog͡bo/
Cow/Cattle	Ehi	/efi/
Chick	Nwa Ọkụkọ	/ŋʷa ɔkʊkɔ/
Cock	Oke Ọkpa	/oke ɔk͡pa/
Dog	Nkịta	/nkɪta/

Donkey	Jakị	/d͡ʒaki/
Dove	nduru ala	/nduru ala/
Duck	Ọbọgwụ	/ɔbɔgʷʊ/
Female goat	Nne ewu	/nne ewu/
Fowl/Chicken	Ọkụkọ	/ɔkʊkɔ/
Goat	Ewu	/ewu/
Gold fish	Azụ ọlaedo	/azʊ ɔlaedo/
Guinea pig	Oke Bekee	/oke bekee/
Hen	Nnekwu	/nnekʷu/
Horse	Ịnyịya	/ɪɲja/
Male goat	Mkpị	/mk͡pɪ/
Parrot	Icheku	/it͡ʃeku/

Chapter 14

Articulatory Phonetics (Amụmàmụ Mkpọpụta Ụdaasụsụ)

The 28 consonant phonemes of Igbo language are categorized into:

- 10 oral stops {/p, b, t, d, k, g, kʷ, gʷ, k͡p and g͡ɓ/}
- 5 nasal stops {/m, n, ɲ, ŋ and ŋʷ /}
- 2 affricates {/ t͡ʃ, d͡ʒ/} and
- 7 fricatives {/f, v, s, z, ʃ, ɣ and h/}
- 2 glides {/j and w/}
- 1 Approximant central rhotic {/ɹ/} and
- 1 Approximant lateral {/l/}

When there is vibration, the sounds produced are called **voiced consonant sounds (ụdamputa Mgbochiume)**. When there is no vibration, the sounds produced are called **voiceless consonant sounds (Udaogbi Mgbochiume)**.

- **The voiced consonants (u̩damputa Mgbochiume):** /n/ /m/ /l/ /j/ /ɲ/ /ŋʷ/ /ŋ/ /z/ /w/ /v/ /dʒ/ /g/ /gʷ/ /ɡ͡b/ /d/ /b/ /ɦ/ /ɣ/ /ɹ/

- **The voiceless consonants (U̩daogbi Mgbochiume):** /p/ /t/ /s/ /k/ /kʷ/ /k͡p/ /f/ /ʃ/ /tʃ/

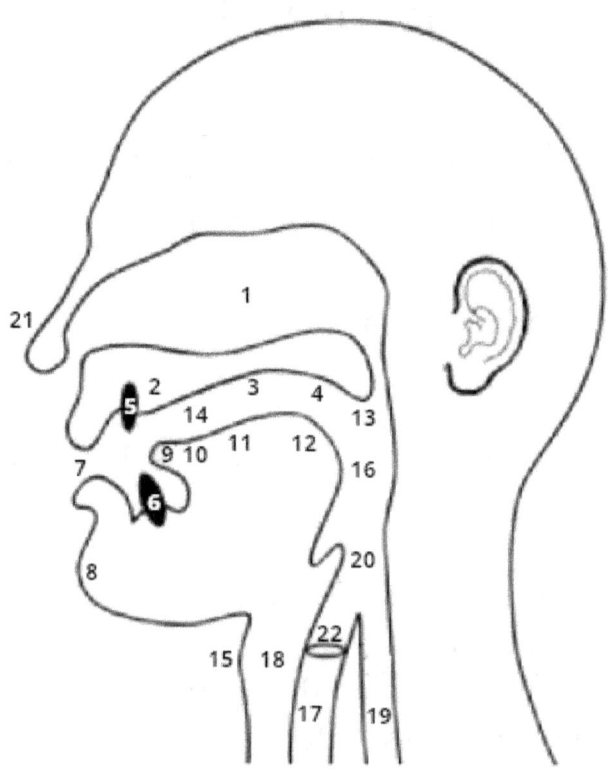

List of the parts shown (Aha na mkpo̩pu̩ta ihe osise)

English   **Igbo**
1. *Nasal cavity*   Uju imi
2. *Alveolar ridge* Anyu̩ru̩

3. *Hard palate* — Akpo ihu
4. *Velum/soft palate* — Akpo ime
5. *Upper Teeth* — Eze elu
6. *Lower teeth* — Eze ala
7. *Lips* — Egbugbere Ọnụ
8. *Jaw* — Agba
9. *Tongue tip* — Ọnụ ire
10. *Front of tongue* — Ihu ire
11. *Blade of tongue* — Ugbo ire
12. *Back of Tongue* — Azụ ire
13. *Uvula* — Ụvụla
14. *Oral/Buccal Cavity* — Uju Ọnụ
15. *Adam's apple* — Eko akpịrị
16. *Pharynx* — Nkọlọ
17. *Trachea/Wind pipe* — Opi akpịrị
18. *Larynx* — Ogworo
19. *Esophagus* — Ọwa nri
20. *Epiglottis* — Asha
21. *Nose* — Imi
22. *Vocal cord* — Mkpọụda

The Manner of articulating the consonant sounds has to do with how the vocal tract (the oral cavity, nasal cavity, and pharynx) is narrowed or blocked during production. The manner of articulation is categorized into: **stops, fricatives, affricates, nasal, lateral, glide and rhotic.**

The stops (Ụdaike): - These are sounds produced with a total blockage of airflow or momentary blocking (occlusion) of some part of the oral cavity.

STOP	Voiced	b	d	g	gw	gb
	Voiceless (Udaogbi)	p	t	k	kw	kp

Fricative (Ụdashịị): - these consonant sounds are produced by bringing the mouth into position to block the passage of the airstream, but not making complete closure, so that air moving through the mouth generates audible friction.

FRICATIVE	Voiceless (Udaogbi)	f	s	sh		
	Voiced	v	Z		Gh	h

Affricate (Ụdachịị): - Affricates also called semiplosives are consonant sounds that begin as a stop (sound with complete obstruction of the breath stream) and concludes with a fricative (sound with incomplete closure and a sound of friction).

AFFRICATE	Voiceless (Udaogbi)	ch
	Voiced	j

Nasal (Ụdaimi): - Nasal, also called a nasal occlusive or nasal stop in contrast with an oral stop or nasalized consonant, is an occlusive consonant produced with a lowered velum, allowing air to escape freely through the nose. The vast majority of consonants are oral consonants.

| NASAL | Voiced | m | N | ny | ṅ | Nw |

Lateral (Ụdalịị): - lateral consonant sounds are produced by raising the tip of the tongue against the roof of the mouth so that the airstream flows past one or both sides of the tongue.

| LATERAL | Voiced | L |

Glides (Ụdayịị): Glides are speech sounds produced when the airstream is frictionless and is modified by the position of the tongue and the lips.

| GLIDE | Voiced | y | w |

Rhotic (Ụdarịị): Rhotic are consonant speech sounds produced when the front part of the tongue approaches the upper gum, or the tongue-tip is curled back towards the roof of the mouth ("retroflexion"). No or little friction can be heard, and there is no momentary closure of the vocal tract.

| RHOTIC | Voiced | R |

The process of speech production
Bilabial sounds (Nke Egbugbere Ọnụ abụọ): Bilabial sounds involve the upper and lower lips. In the production of a bilabial

sound, the lips come into contact with each other to form an effective constriction. The consonant sounds that belong to this group are:

m   b   kp   gb   p

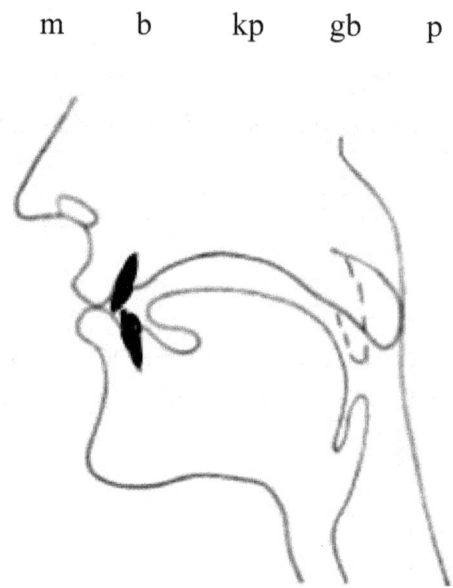

Labiodental sounds (Nke Egbugbere Ọnụ na Eze): Labiodental sounds involve the lower lip (labial) and upper teeth (dental) coming into contact with each other to form an effective constriction in the vocal tract. The consonant sounds that belong to this group are:

f   and   v

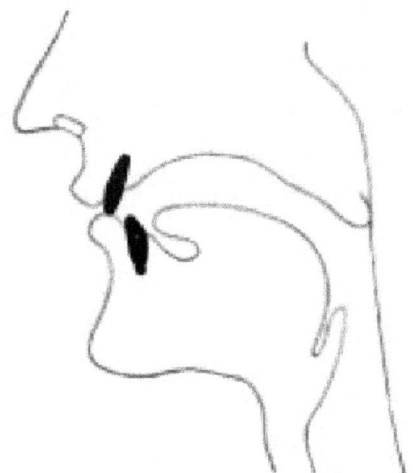

Alveolar (Nke Anyụrụ na Akpo): Alveolar consonants are consonant sounds that are produced with the tongue close to or touching the ridge behind the teeth on the roof of the mouth. The name comes from alveoli - the sockets of the teeth. The consonant sounds that belong to this group are:

    d,   t,   s,   z,   n,   r and   l

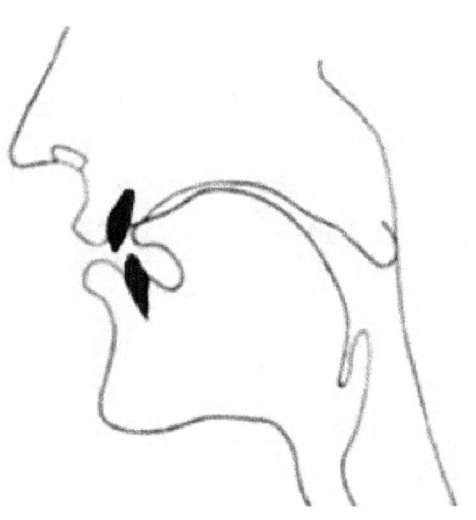

Palatoaveolar sound (Nke Akpo ihu na akpo ime): are consonant sounds produced by raising the blade, or front, of the tongue toward or against the hard palate just behind the alveolar ridge (the gums). The consonant sounds that belong to this group are:

    ch   j   sh   ny

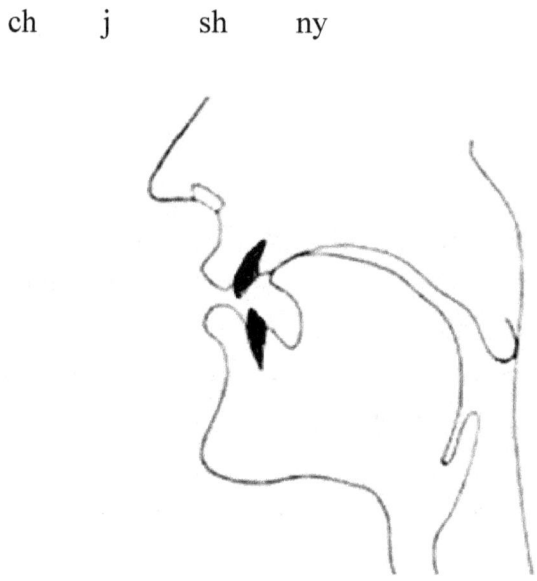

Velar (Egbugbere Ọnụ na Akpo): consonant that is pronounced with the back part of the tongue against the soft palate, also known as the velum, which is the back part of the roof of the mouth. The consonant sounds that belong to this group are divided into plain and labial subgroups.

Plain: g   k   gh   y   ṅ

Labial: gw   kw   nw

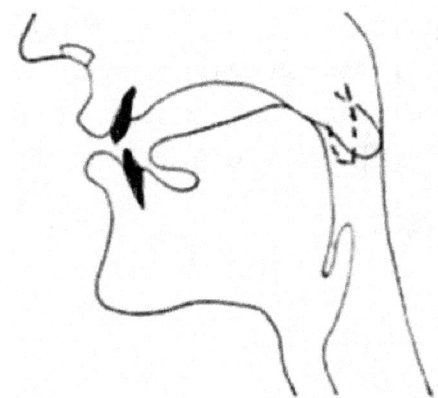

Labial Velar (Kemkpọnegbugbere Ọnụ): Truly doubly articulated labial-velars include the stops [k͡p, ɡ͡b and w]. To pronounce them, one must attempt to say the velar consonants but then close their lips for the bilabial component, and then release the lips.

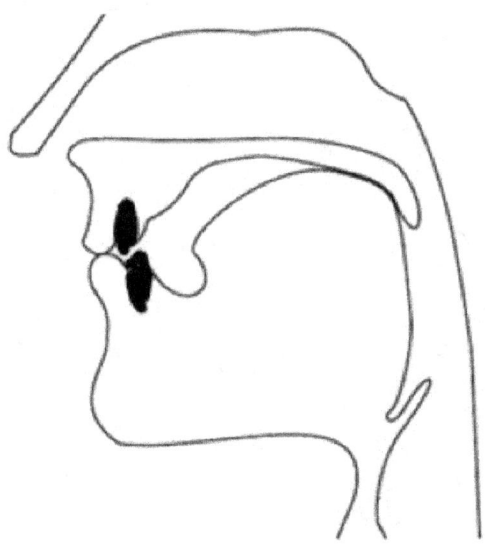

Glottal (Keekoapiri): Glottal sound is a sound produced when the air passes through the open space (glottis) between the vocal cords. It is the sound produced without the active use of the tongue and other part of the mouth. The consonant sound that belongs to this group is: /h/.

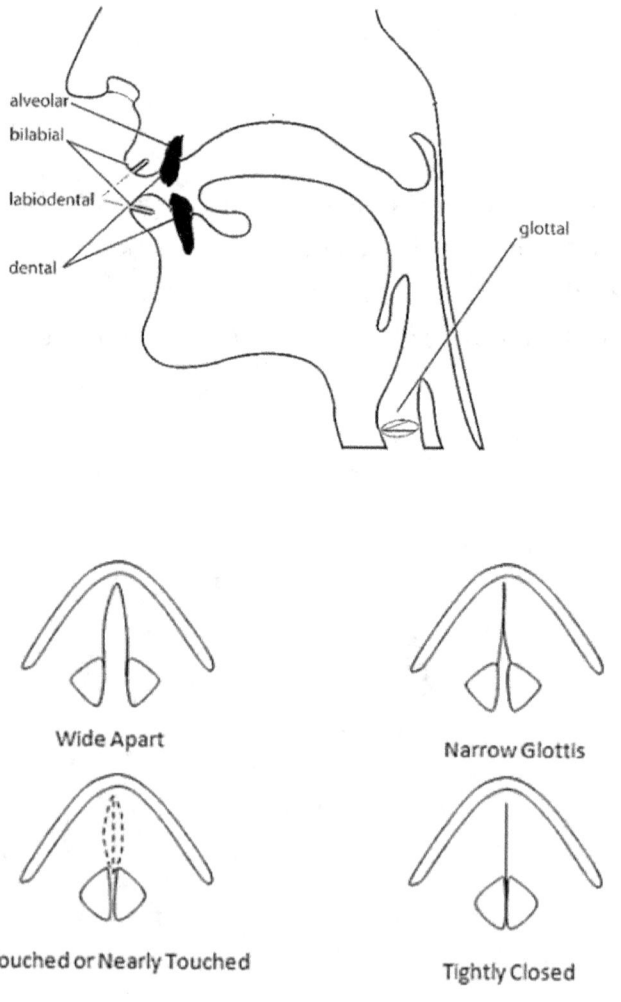

Four different states of the glottis adapted from Peter Roach.

Part Three:

Morphology of Igbo Linguistic (Amụmàmụ Mkpụrụasụsụ nke Mmụta Asụsụ Igbo)

Chapter 15

The nature of Igbo Morpheme (Amụmàmụ Ọdịdị nke Mkpụrụasụsụ Igbo)

Morphology is the study of words, how they are formed, and their relationship to other words in the same language. It analyzes the structure of words and parts of words such as stems, root words, prefixes, and suffixes.

Morpheme (mkpụrụasụsụ) is the smallest linguistic unit that contains an element of a word that cannot be divided into smaller parts. They are a distinct grammatical unit of a language by which meaningful words are formed. A morpheme (mkpụrụasụsụ) is not a word. The difference between a morpheme (mkpụrụasụsụ) and a word is that a morpheme (mkpụrụasụsụ) sometimes does not stand alone, but a word on this definition always stands alone.

Examples of morpheme (mkpụrụasụsụ) within Igbo words:

Word	*Morpheme (mkpụrụasụsụ)*	*No. of Morpheme*
Bịara	[bị] + [a] + [ra]	3 - (atọ)
Cheta	[che] + [ta]	2 - (abụọ)
Chọpụtara	[chọ] + [pụ] + [ta] + [ra]	4 - (anọ)
Di	[di]	1 - (otu)
Dibịa	[di] + [bị] + [a]	3 - (atọ)
Ghọtakwa	[ghọ] + [ta] + [kwa]	3 - (atọ)

Ma	[m] + [a]	2 - (abụọ)
Mata	[m] + [a] + [ta]	3 - (atọ)
Metụtara	[m] + [e] + [tụ] + [ta] + [ra]	5 - (ise)
Mgbochiume	[m] + [gbo] + [chi] + [ume]	4 - (anọ)
Nkuzi	[nku] + [zi]	2 - (abụọ)
Nwannem	[nwa] + [nne] + [m]	3 - (atọ)
Ọmụmaatụ	[ọ] + [mụ] + [ma] + [a] + [tụ]	5 - (ise)
bụ	[bụ]	1 - (otu)
Zipụ	[zi] + [pụ]	2 - (abụọ)

The difference between morpheme (mkpụrụasụsụ) and phoneme (mkpụrụụdaasụsụ)

	Morpheme (mkpụrụasụsụ)	Phoneme
1.	*It is the smallest grammatical unit from which words are formed.*	*It is a unit of sound that can distinguish one word from another.*
2.	*It does have individual meaning and can stand alone when separated from words or in a sentence.*	*It does not have individual meaning. It rather has individual sound which is found within words.*

Identification of Igbo morphemes (mkpụrụasụsụ):

Since morphemes (mkpụrụasụsụ) are the smallest grammatical unit from which words are formed. It is important to understand how it differs from other linguistic features (like phonemes or words) by knowing certain conditions that qualifies some lexical units as morphemes (mkpụrụasụsụ). Here are five basic features of morphemes (mkpụrụasụsụ) that distinguish them from other linguistic elements:

1. Igbo morpheme (mkpụrụasụsụ) is a part of a word or a word that has meaning.
2. It has almost the same stable meaning in different verbal environments.
3. It cannot be divided into smaller meaningful segments without changing its meaning or rendering it meaningless.

(A). The following are examples of morphemes (mkpụrụasụsụ) that are a part of a word or a word that has meaning.

Word	Morphemes (mkpụrụasụsụ) and Meaning
Bịa	[bị] *(live)* + [a] *(impersonal pronoun)*
Cheta	[che] *(think)* + [ta] *(past tense suffix)*
Chọpụta	[chọ] *(find)* + [pụ] *(go)* + [ta] *(past tense suffix)*
Ghọta	[ghọ] *(get/catch)* + [ta] *(past tense suffix)*
Metụta	[me] *(do/take action)* + [tụ] *(about)*
Nwannem	[nwa] *(child)* + [nne] *(mother)* + [m] *(mine/me)*

(B). The following are examples of Igbo morphemes (mkpụrụasụsụ) that have almost the same stable meaning in different verbal environments.

Using the morpheme (mkpụrụasụsụ) – '*che*' meaning hold on, guard, think

Word	Morphemes (mkpụrụasụsụ)	Meaning
Cheta	[che] + [ta]	remember
Chere	[che] + [re]	wait/hold on
Chebe	[che] + [be]	protect

Echiche   [E] + [chi] + [che}   ideas

Using the morpheme (mkpụrụasụsụ) – '*me*' meaning do
Metụ   [me] + [tụ]   touch
Mebe   [me] + [be}   keep doing/going on
Meta   [me] + [ta]   do (it) well
Mechie [me] + [chi] + [e]   close/shut
Emeka [e] + [me] + [ka]   (has) done so well
Emeniike [e] + [me] + [ni] [i] + [ke]   not done by force
Mebie [me] + [bi] + [e]   ruin, (do) damage

Using the morpheme (mkpụrụasụsụ) – '*Gho*' meaning get
Ghọta   [ghọ] + [ta]   understand
Ghọrọ   [ghọ] + [rọ]   catch

(C). The following are examples that show that morphemes (mkpụrụasụsụ) cannot be divided into smaller meaningful segments without changing its meaning or rendering it meaningless.

Word	*Morphemes (mkpụrụasụsụ)*	
Bịara	[bị] + [a] + [ra]	3 - indivisible
Cheta	[che] + [ta]	2 - indivisible
Chọpụtara	[chọ] + [pụ] + [ta] + [ra]	4 - indivisible
Di	[di]	1 - indivisible
Dibịa	[di] + [bị] + [a]	3 - indivisible
Ghọtakwa	[ghọ] + [ta] + [kwa]	3 - indivisible
Ma	[m] + [a]	2 - indivisible
Mata	[m] + [a] + [ta]	3 - indivisible
Mkpụrụasụsụ	[m] + [kpụ] + [rụ] + [a] + [sụ] + [sụ]	6 - indivisible
Mgbochiume	[m] + [gbo] + [chi] + [ume]	4 - indivisible

Nkuzi	[nku] + [zi]	2 - indivisible
Nwannem	[nwa] + [nne] + [m]	3 - indivisible
Ọmụmaatụ	[ọ] + [mụ] + [ma] + [a] + [tụ]	5 - indivisible
bụ	[bụ]	1 - indivisible
Zipụ	[zi] + [pụ]	2 - indivisible

Illustrations below show that attempt to further divide Igbo morpheme (mkpụrụasụsụ) will either render that morpheme (mkpụrụasụsụ) meaningless or change its meaning to something different.

(a). Unit of Morpheme (mkpụrụasụsụ) [nwa]
  Division [nw] + [a]

Result [nw] *is meaningless while [a] as a separate entity assume the position of an impersonal pronoun.*

(b). Unit of Morpheme (mkpụrụasụsụ) [nne]
  Division [n] + [n] + [e]

Result *the two* [n]*s are meaningless while [a] as a separate entity assumes the position of an impersonal pronoun.*

(c). Unit of Morpheme (mkpụrụasụsụ) [ume]
  Division [u] + [m] + [e]

Result *the two [u] are meaningless while [m] and [e] as separate entities assume the position of personal and impersonal pronoun respectively.*

Characteristics of Igbo morpheme (mkpụrụasụsụ):

(A). In Igbo sentences (ahịrịokwu), a pronoun that can stand alone can double as a morpheme (mkpụrụasụsụ) as well as a word. For example:

Sentence	Meaning	Pronoun/Morpheme
A sara efere.	Someone *did the dishes*	a
E siri nri.	*Someone cooked food*	e
Ị mere m ihe ọma.	*You did me a favor*	i
Ị bu ezigbo mmadu.	*You are a kind person*	ị
O buuru ụzọ.	*He/she took the lead*	o
Ọ mara ezigbo mma	*He/she is so beautiful*	ọ
M ga-abia.	*I will come*	m
Ada gwara ya	*Ada told him/her*	ya
Eze gwara ha.	*Eze told them.*	ha
Anyị bụ ụmụnne	*We are siblings*	anyị
Gịnị bụ aha gị?	*What is your name?*	gị
Unu amaghị Obi.	*You (people) don't know Obi*	unu.

(B). Igbo alphabet (Abidịị), that can stand alone and have stable meaning can double as a morpheme (mkpụrụasụsụ). Igbo alphabet has two divisions – vowels and consonants. Igbo vowels can double as morpheme (mkpụrụasụsụ) because they can stand alone as lexical unit and have meaning. A look at the preceding example shows that the following vowels are morphemes (mkpụrụasụsụ) as well.

      a   e   i   ị   o   ọ

Six out of eight Igbo vowels qualify as morphemes (mkpụrụasụsụ) as you can see from the above examples. There are two Igbo vowels that do not qualify as morpheme (mkpụrụasụsụ) because they do not have meaning when they stand alone. They are:

u   and   ụ

Similarly, semi-vowels that are part of Igbo consonant have only one among the two (m and n) that qualifies as a morpheme (mkpụrụasụsụ). This is because while one would stand alone and still have meaning, the other does not have meaning as standalone. The semivowel that qualifies as morpheme (mkpụrụasụsụ) is:

m

The semivowel that does not qualify as a morpheme (mkpụrụasụsụ) because of lack of meaning is:

n

Chapter 16

The Classification of Igbo Morpheme (Nkewasị Mkpụrụasụsụ Igbo)

Morphemes (mkpụrụasụsụ) are the smallest meaningful lexical item in a language. It is the smallest meaningful and syntactical or grammatical unit of a language that cannot be divided without changing its actual meaning. There are two ways of classifying morpheme (mkpụrụasụsụ):

1. *Free Morpheme* (Mkpụrụasụsụ Nnọrọonwe)
2. *Bound Morpheme* (Mkpụrụasụsụ Ndabe)

Free Morpheme (Mkpụrụasụsụ Nnọrọonwe): Free morpheme (mkpụrụasụsụ) is a morpheme (mkpụrụasụsụ) that has individual meaning and can be formed independently. For example: bi *(live)*, bụ *(is)*, dì *(for)*, dí *(husband)*, ma *(know)*, jì *(have)*, jí *(yam)*, etc. All of the words have individual meanings and are free morphemes (mkpụrụasụsụ). Morphemes (mkpụrụasụsụ) such as *anuri, happy, nwoke, man, papa, father, aka, hand,* among others can stand on their own as independent words. Free morpheme (mkpụrụasụsụ) in Igbo language can be either one letter of Igbo alphabet (such as a, e, i, ị, o, ọ or m) or indivisible grammatical unit (such as bi *(live)*, bụ *(is)*, dì *(for)*, dí *(husband)*, ma *(know)*, jì *(have)*, jí *(yam)*, anyị *(we)*, okwu *(word)*, ha *(they/them)*, ụmụ *(Kids/Children)*, nne *(mother)*, nna *(father)*, etc). Free morphemes (mkpụrụasụsụ) can be categorized into two sub-types. They are: Lexical morphemes (mkpụrụasụsụ) or Grammatical/functional morpheme (mkpụrụasụsụ).

Lexical morphemes: these are morphemes (mkpụrụasụsụ) that convey the major content or meaning of a message. They specify things, qualities or events spoken about. To identify a lexical morpheme (mkpụrụasụsụ), ask yourself this: "If this morpheme (mkpụrụasụsụ) was removed from the sentence, statement or message, would I not be able to understand the main message of this sentence?" If the answer is yes, then you have a lexical morpheme (mkpụrụasụsụ).

Functional morphemes: Functional morphemes also known as *grammatical morphemes* are morphemes (mkpụrụasụsụ) that do not convey the major content or meaning of a message, but rather help the message with function words. To identify a lexical morpheme, ask yourself this: "If this morpheme (mkpụrụasụsụ) was removed from the sentence, statement or message, would I still be able to understand the main message of this sentence?" If the answer is yes, then you have a functional morpheme.

Bound Morphemes (*Mkpụrụasụsụ Ndabe*): These are morphemes that do not have independent meanings of their own. They cannot form words without the help of free morphemes (mkpụrụasụsụ). Morphemes (mkpụrụasụsụ) like *ghi,* indicating negation, *beghi, ra,* meaning *past ga-* indicating *futurity, chara,* indicating completion, *li and ri,* indicating intensity, are always attached to free morphemes or free forms. It entails that bound morphemes depend on the form to which they are attached to derive meaning. Bound morphemes can be categorized into two sub-classes. They are: Bound roots (usually Isingwaa) and Affixes (mgbakwunye).

Bound Roots: Bound roots are those morphemes that have lexical meaning when they are included in other bound morphemes to form the content words. An example of bound roots is infinitive verb (Isingwaa).

An infinitive verb (Isingwaa) is a verb form that functions as a noun or is used with auxiliary verbs, and that names the action or state without specifying the subject. In Igbo language, the letter "i" and "i" plus the root verb comprise the infinitive form of verb. For example:

English	Igbo root verb	*English*	Igbo root verb
to be	ịbu/ịdị	to bring	iweta
to buy	ịzụta	to call	ịkpọ
to chew	ịta	to come	ịbịa
to cook	isi nri	to cry	ibe akwa
to dance	ịgba egwu	to do	ime
to drink	ịṅu	to eat	iri (nri)
to enter	ịbanye/ịbata	to find/look	ịchọ/chọta
to follow	isoro	to forget	ichefu
to fry	ighe	to get	inweta
to give	inye	to go	ịga
to have/own	inwe	to hear	ịnụ
to hold	ijide	to know	ịma

to laugh	ịchi (chi a)	*to learn*	ịmụta
to leave	ịhapụ	*to listen*	ige ntị
to look	ile (anya)	*to mark*	ịka (akara)
to get out	ịpụta	*to play*	igwu egwu
to pray	ikpe ekpere	*to read*	ịgụ
to remember	icheta	*to run*	ịgba ọsọ
to say	ikwu (okwu)	*to see*	ịhụ
to sell	ire (ahịa)	*to bathe*	ịsa ahụ
to sing	ịgụụ abụ/ ịbụụ abụ	*to sit*	ịnọdu
to sleep	ịrahụ (ura)	*to speak*	ịsụ/ikwu
to stand	iguzo/ikuli	*to stay*	ịnọ
to swallow	ilo	*to take*	iwere
to teach	ikuzi	*to tell*	ịgwa
to think	iche echiche	*to throw*	ịtu
to touch	ịmetụ	*to understand*	ịghọta
to wait	ichere	*to walk*	ịga ije
to wash	ịsa	*to wear*	iyi
to work	ịrụ	*to write*	ide

Chapter 17

Morphological Process of Igbo Word (Usoro Mkpụrụasụsụ nke Mkpụrụokwu)

Morphology is the study of morphemes and their arrangements in forming words. The morphological process is the process of changing the form and function of a word to fit a statement or idea, sometimes to the degree of changing the meaning and/or grammatical function. Morphological process in Igbo language can be divided into seven kinds: Affixation, Clipping, Compounding, Borrowing/Loanword, Reduplication, Blending, Acronyms.

In this chapter, we will focus on affixation because of how broad its content is in Igbo language and in the following chapter we will discuss the remaining six kinds of morphological process under word process and formation.

AFFIXATION
Affixes: Affixes are those bound morphemes that naturally attached to different types of words and are used to change the meaning or function of those words.

Agglutination is a notable feature of Igbo language. The conjugation of verbs, for example, is done by adding different prefixes or suffixes to the root of the verb: *metutara*, which means "has/that affected", is formed by *"metu"* (indicates present tense "touch"), (root of the verb *"me"* → do), tara (indicates past tense, in this case, "touched/affected"). Generally, most Igbo verbs come with affixes or other nominals as part of their complex e.g.

bá	-	*enter*
bátà	-	*enter into*
cha	-	*cut*
chapụ	-	*cut out*
chọ	-	*look for*
chọta	-	*find*
gwá	–	*tell*
gwáá	-	*mix*
ma	-	*know*
maka	-	*because*
ri	-	*eat*
riri	-	*ate*
zi	-	*inform*
zipu	-	*send (a person)*

Affixes can be categorized into five sub-classes according to their position in the word and function in a phrase or sentence. They are:
    a. Prefixes (Ngaaniihu)
    b. Infixes (Nnọnaetiti)
    c. Suffixes (Nsonaazụ)
    d. Derivational (Nsonaazu Mgbanwe)

e. Inflectional (Nsonaazụ ntụaka)
f. Enclitic (Nsokwụnye)

SUB-CLASS 1

Prefixes (ngaaniihu): Prefixes are bound morphemes (mkpụrụasụsụ) included at the beginning of different types of words. In Igbo language prefixation is verb-based. There is no other word class that undergoes this kind of morphological process. Prefixes in Igbo are infinitive and participle markers that are attached to verb roots. They normally appear as bound morphemes (mkpụrụasụsụ) to the verb root in the following manner:

Participles	-	Òmekàngwaà
Infinitives	-	Mfinitiivu
Gerund	-	Jerọndụ
Noun agent	-	Ahaome/Omee
Noun instrument	-	Ahamme/Mmee

Examples with *Participles* (Òmekàngwaà):

Prefix (nganiihu)	*Verb root* (Isingwaa)	*New word* (Mkpụrụokwuọhụru)	*Meaning* (Ihe ọ pụtata)
a	bụ	abụ	*song*
a	da	Ada	*first daughter*
a	kpa	Akpa	*bag*
a	gba	Agba	*jaw*
e	de	Ede	*cocoyam*

181

e	nyo	Enyo	*mirror*
e	je	Eje	*go (ing)*
e	ti	Eti	*beat (ing)*
a	nwụ	anwụ	*sun*
a	gwụ	agwụ	*maniac*

Examples with infinitives (Mfinitiivu):

Prefix (nganiihu)	**Verb root** (Isingwaa)	**Infinitives** (Mfinitiivu)	**Meaning** (Ihe ọ pụtata)
ị	ba	ịbá	*to enter*
ị	da	ịda	*to fall*
ị	kpa	ịkpa	*to discuss*
ị	gba	ịgba	*to play/dane*
i	de	ide	*to write*
i	nyo	inyo	*to peek*
i	ke	ike (wa)	*to divide*
ị	ma	ịmá	*to know*
i	re	irè	*to sell*
i	zu	izu	*to device*

Examples with *Gerund* (Jerọndụ):

Prefix (nganiihu)	**Verb root** (Isingwaa)	**Infinitives** (Mfinitivu)	**Gerund** (Jerondu)	**Meaning** (Ihe ọ pụtata)
o	ri	ri	oriri	*eating/feasting*
ọ	nyụ	nya	ọnyụnya	*driving*
ọ	ṅụ	ṅụ	ọṅụṅụ	*drinking*

ọ	dị	da	ọdịda	*falling*
o	di	de	odide	*writing*
ọ	gụ	gụ	ọgụgụ	*reading*
o	ri	re	orire	*selling*
ọ	mụ	mụ	ọmụmụ	*learning/bearing*
ọ	hụ	hụ	ahụhụ	*roasting*
ọ	sụ	sọ	ọsụsọ	*sweating*
o	bi	bi	obibi	*living (home)*
o	ti	ti	otiti	*beating*

Example with Noun agent (Ahaomee/Omee):

Prefix (nganiihu)	***Two verb root*** (Isingwaa abụọ)	***Noun Agent*** (Ahaomee/Omee)	***Meaning*** (Ihe ọ pụtata)
o	me + e	Omee	*(noun) agent*
o	de + e	Ode	*writer*
o	le + e	Olee	*where/how many*
o	me + e	Omee	*doer*
ọ	ga + a	ọgaa	*boss*
ọ	gba + a	ọgbaa	*shooter*
ọ	kụ + ụ	ọkụụ	*planter/sower*
ọ	sụ + ụ	ọsụụ	*speaker/cutter*
ọ	ṅụ + ụ	ọṅụụ	*drinker*
o	je + e	Ojee	*traveler/goer*

Example with Noun instrument (Ahammee/Mmee):

Prefix (nganiihu)	Verb root (Isingwaa)	Complement (Mmeju)	Ahamme/Mmee (Noun Instrument)	Translation (Ntụgharị)
m	gba	mmiri	mgbammiri	*jug*
m	pa	naka	mpanaka	*hand lamp*
m	kpa	isi	mkpaisi	*scissors*
m	gba	ama	mgbaama	*revealer*
n	che	ndo	nchendo	*sun protector*
n	ti	mkpu	nti mkpu	*exclaimer*
n	ku	ikuku	nku ikuku	*fan*
n	de	akwa	nde akwa	*iron*
n	tụ	oyi	ntụ oyi	*air conditioner*
n	gụ	ọnụ	ngụ ọnụ	*counter*

SUB-CLASS 2

Infixes (Nnoṇaetiti): In linguistics, an infix is an affix inserted inside a word stem. A word stem is an existing word or the core of a family of words. It contrasts with adfix, a rare term for an affix attached to the outside of a stem such as a prefix or suffix.

In morphology, an infix is a word element (a type of affix) that can be inserted within the base form of a word—rather than at its beginning or end—to create a new word or intensify meaning. The process of inserting an infix is called infixation. There are no infixes that exist in the English language.

In Igbo morphology, an infix occurs within two words of the same morphemes (mkpụrụasụsụ) or words of the same form. The two morphemes (mkpụrụasụsụ) or words that are joined together by an infix in Igbo morphological process are usually verbs, nouns or adverb.

Examples of Infixes (nnọnetiti)

Infix (nnọnetiti)	Verb/stem (Ngwaa/ okwu)	reduplication (Mmụba)	New word (Okwu ọhụ)	Translation (Ntụghari)
d	aga	aga + aga	agadaga	*hardy/robust*
r	aka	aka + aka	akaraka	*fate/destiny*
m	aṅụ	aṅụ + aṅụ	aṅụmaṅụ	*act of drinking*
r	apị	apị + apị	apịrapị	*man-made*
m	asụ	asụ + asụ	asụmasụ	*act of speaking*
m	ata	ata + ata	atamata	*act of chewing*
l	ebe	ebe + ebe	ebelebe	*horrifying/ shocking*
m	echi	echi + echi	echimechi	*crowning*
m	ede	ede + ede	edemede	*writing*
m	ekwu	ekwu + ekwu	ekwumekwu	*speech making*
r	ekwu	ekwu + ekwu	ekwurekwu	*talkative*
m	eri	eri + eri	erimeri	*act of eating*
m	esi	esi + esi	esimesi	*act of cooking*
m	eti	eti + eti	etimeti	*act of shouting*
da	mba	mba + mba	mbadamba	*wide/width*
m	oko	oko + oko	ókómókó	*proudful*
m	oko	oko + oko	òkómòkò	*troublemaker*
ka	ome	ome + ome	omekaome	*robber/criminal*

SUB-CLASS 3

Suffixes (Nsonaazụ): Suffixes are those bound morphemes included at the end of different types of words. They can add meaning, and usually determine the part of speech of a word. In Igbo language, morpheme and verbs can have suffix. Igbo language as a tonal language has also been described as a verb language. In the morphology of the Igbo language, Igbo suffixes make constant reference to the verb forms in the language. For example:

Suffix (nsonaazụ)	Verb/Word (Ngwaa/ Mkpụrụokwu)	Affixation (Mgbakwụnye)	New word (Okwu ọhụ)	Translation (Ntụgharị)
ra	ba	ba + ra	bara	*entered*
re	be	be + re	bere	*perched*
ra	cha	cha + ra	chara	*cut*
re	che	che + re	chere	*thought*
ra	da	da + ra	dara	*fell*
e	di	di + e	die	*endure*
ọ	kọ	kọ + ọ	kọọ	*scratch*
ọ	kpọ	kpọ + ọ	kpọọ	*call*
e	me	me + e	mee	*do*
rụ	mụ	mụ + rụ	mụrụ	*learned*
ọ	rụ	rụ + ọ	rụọ	*do (work)*
ọ	sụ	sụ + ọ	sụọ	*speak*
ra	za	za + ra	zara	*answered*
e	zi	zi + e	zie	*send/inform*
ri	zi	zi + ri	ziri	*sent/informed*

SUB-CLASS 4

Derivational morphemes: Derivational morphemes create new words from existing words, i.e. new words are derived from their use. Derivational morphemes produce entirely new lexemes, highly productive, belong to the open class system and can bring about a change in the word class or modify the meaning of the word. They may be either prefixes or suffixes.

There are two primary types of derivational affixes in Igbo language, namely:

1. *Derivational suffix* (Nsonaazụ Mgbanwe) and
2. *Extentional suffix* (Nsonaazụ Mgbatị).

Derivational Affixes (**Nsonaazụ Mgbanwe**)**:** Derivational morphemes (mkpụrụasụsụ mgbanwe) make new words by changing their meaning or different grammatical categories. In other words, derivational suffix (Nsonazụ Mgbanwe) forms new words with a meaning and category distinct through the addition of affixes.

In order to identify a derivational morpheme (mkpụrụasụsụ mgbanwe), ask this question: "If this morpheme (mkpụrụasụsụ mgbanwe) was added, would it change the part of speech of this word?" If the answer is yes, then you have a derivational morpheme. For example:

Suffix (nsonaazụ mgbanwe)	*Verb/Word* (Ngwaa/ Mkpụrụokwu)	*Affixation* (Mgbakwụnye)	*New word* (Okwu ọhụ)	*Translation* (Ntụghari)
a	ba	ba + a	baa	*enter*

e	be	be + e	bee	*slice*
o	bu	bu + o	buo	*carry*
ọ	bụ	bụ + ọ	bụọ	*dissect*
ọ	chọ	chọ + ọ	chọọ	*seek*
ọ	dụ	dụ + ọ	dụọ	*advise*
e	fe	fe + e	fee	*fly*
a	gba	gba + a	gbaa	*kick/shoot*
ọ	kpụ	kpụ + ọ	kpụọ	*mould/form*
o	ku	ku + o	kuo	*fetch*

Derivational morpheme can be categorized into two sub-classes. They are:
1. Class-maintaining derivational morphemes
2. Class-changing derivational morphemes

1. Class-Maintaining Derivational Morphemes: Class-maintaining derivational morphemes are usually produced in a derived form of the same class as the root, and they don't change the class of the parts of speech. Class maintaining derivational morpheme does not alter the word class but modifies its meaning, most prefixes are class maintaining. For example; if a verb class undergoes an affixation and still remains a verb, it means there is no change of class. Thus, it is a class maintaining derivation. Inflectional affixes are common.

Suffix (nsonaazụ mgbanwe)	*Verb/Word* (Ngwaa/ Mkpụrụokwu)	*Affixation* (Mgbakwụnye)	*New Verb* (Ngwaa ọhụ)	*Translation* (Ntụgharị)
a	ba	ba + a	baa	*enter*
e	be	be + e	bee	*slice*

o	bu	bu + o	buo	*carry*
e	ke	ke + e	kee	*divide*
ọ	chọ	chọ + ọ	chọọ	*seek*
ọ	dụ	dụ + ọ	dụọ	*advise*
e	fe	fe + e	fee	*fly*
a	gba	gba + a	gbaa	*kick/shoot*
ọ	kpụ	kpụ + ọ	kpụọ	*mould/form*
e	che	che + e	chee	*think*

2. *Class-Changing Derivational Morphemes*: In contrast to Class-maintaining derivational morphemes, Class-changing derivational morphemes usually produce a derived form of the other class from the root. Class changing derivational morpheme does not alter the word class but modifies its meaning. For example, if a verb class undergoes an affixation and change from being a verb to noun of other part of speech after suffixation or prefixation. It means there is a change of class. Thus, it is a class changing derivation.

Infix (nnọnetiti)	**Verb** (Ngwaa)	**New word** (Okwu ọhụ)	**Translation** (Ntụghari)	**Part of Speech** (Nkejiasụsụ)
d	aga	agadaga	*hardy/robust*	adjective
m	aṅụ	aṅụmaṅụ	*alcoholism*	noun
r	apị	apịrapị	*man-made*	adjective
m	ata	atamata	*mastication*	noun
l	ebe	ebelebe	*horrifying/ shocking*	adjective
m	echi	echimechi	*crowning*	adjective
m	ede	edemede	*writing*	noun

m	ekwu	ekwumekwu	*speech-making*	noun
r	ekwu	ekwurekwu	*talkative*	adjective
m	eri	erimeri	*feast/banquet*	noun

More class changing derivational morpheme examples

prefix (nganiihu)	*Verb* (Ngwaa)	*New word* (Okwu ọhụ)	*Translation* (Ntụgharị)	*Part of Speech* (Nkejiasụsụ)
ọ	zọ	ọzọ	*again*	adverb
ọ	zọ	ọzọ	*next*	preposition
ọ	jọọ	ọjọọ	*badly*	adverb
n	cha	ncha	*all*	adverb
a	la	ala	*down*	preposition
ta	ta	tata	*today*	adverb
e	chi	echi	*tomorrow*	adverb
m	ma	mma	*well*	adverb
e	lu	elu	*above*	preposition
n	so	nso	*near*	preposition

suffix (nsonaazụ)	*Verb* (Ngwaa)	*New word* (Okwu ọhụ)	*Translation* (Ntụgharị)	*Part of Speech* (Nkejiasụsụ)
ka	dị	dịka	*as/like*	preposition
ka	ma	maka	*because of*	preposition
pu	tu	tupu	*before*	preposition
o	ru	ruo	*umtil/to*	preposition

Extentional suffix (**Nsonaazụ Mgbatị**): The verb category is very unique in Igbo language. This is because it is characterized with extensive morphological fusions. Extensional suffixes refer to those suffixes that extend the meanings and intention of the Igbo word that they are attached to.

Suffix (nsonaazụ mgbanwe)	*Verb/Word* (Ngwaa/ Mkpụrụokwu)	*Affixation* (Mgbakwụnye)	*New word* (Okwu ọhụ)	*Translation* (Ntụgharị)
ghị	achọ	achọ + ghị	achọghị	*doesn't want*
la	aga	aga + la	agala	*went*
ghị	ahụ	ahụ + ghị	ahụghị	*didn't see*
la	ajụọ	ajụ + ọla	ajụọla	*has asked*
la	akọ	akọ + la	akọla	*has narrated*
ghị	ama	ama + ghị	amaghị	*doesn't know*
la	amụọ	amụ + ọla	amụọla	*has birthed*
la	bee	bee + la	beela	*has sliced*
la	die	die + la	diela	*has endured*
la	eje	eje + la	ejela	*has gone*
ghị	eso	eso + ghị	esoghị	*not following*
la	esu	esu + la	esula	*has burnt*
la	kpụọ	kpụọ + la	kpụọla	*has moulded*
la	kuru	kuru + la	kurula	*has carried*
la	kwuo	kwuo + la	kwuola	*has said*
la	machie	machie + la	machiela	*has banned*
la	merie	merie + la	merela	*has won*
la	mie	mie + la	miela	*has sank*
la	tie	tie + la	tiela	*has beaten*

la	zie	zie + la	ziela	*has sent*
la	zụrụ	zụrụ + la	zụrụla	*has bought*

SUB-CLASS 5

Inflectional suffixes (Nsonaazụ Ntụaka): Inflectional suffix is especially important in Igbo language because it helps in conveying the intended meaning of any expression. It also shows the different forms of verbs that express tone and other aspect in speech using one consonant, one vowel, one semivowel and one syllable or more.

- *one consonant* - otu mgbochiume
- *one vowel* - otu ụdaume
- *one semivowel* - otu myiriụdaume
- *one syllable or more* - otu nkejiokwu maọbụ karịa

Igbo inflectional suffix results into its imperative mood of expression realized by applying the four open vowels suffix with four possible realizations in accordance to vowel harmony rule. The four open vowels are (o or ọ) and (a or e).

Suffix (nsonaazụ mgbanwe)	***Verb/Word*** (Ngwaa/ Mkpụrụokwu)	***Inflected word*** (Mgbakwụnye)	***Igbo sentence*** (Ahịrịokwu)	***Translation*** (Ntụgharị)
ọ	kụ	kụ + ọ	kụọ	*plant*
o	kwu	kwu + o	kwuo	*speak*
e	li	li + e	lie	*bury*
e	me	me + e	mee	*do*
a	mị	mị + a	mịa	*produce*

ọ	mụ	mụ + ọ	mụọ	*learn*
o	pu	pu + o	puo	*bud/shoot*
ọ	pụ	pụ + ọ	pụọ	*go out*
a	rị	rị + a	rịa	*climb*
e	ti	ti + e	tie	*beat*

Inflectional suffix that is added to the root or base of a word to indicate grammatical relationships in terms of tense, aspect or number can be used to mark tense, aspects, mood or negation. This gives variants of an already existing morpheme or word without forming new words. For example, the suffixes: (ra/re), (ro/kọ/tara).

Suffix (nsonaazụ)	*Verb/Word* (Ngwaa/ Mkpụrụokwu)	*Affixation* (Mgbakwụnye)	*New word* (Okwu ọhụ)	*Translation* (Ntụgharị)
ra	ba	ba + ra	bara	*entered*
re	be	be + re	bere	*Perched/sliced*
ra	cha	cha + ra	chara	*Cut/ripe*
re	che	che + re	chere	*thought*
ra	da	da + ra	dara	*fell*
tara	rụ	rụ + tara	rụtara	*did (work)*
tara	sụ	sụ + tara	sụtara	*spoke (well)*
ra	za	za + ra	zara	*answered*
ro	zo	zo + ro	zoro	*to hide*

Inflectional suffix can modify the form of the words or verbs to which they are attached, so that such words fit into the particular syntactic space in an expression. However, they do not change the recognizable meaning of the stem, morpheme, word or verb root.

SUB-CLASS 6

Enclitic (Nsokwụnye): An *enclitic* is a *clitic* that is phonologically joined at the end of a preceding word to form a single unit. It is a monosyllabic word or form that is treated as a suffix of the preceeding word.

In Igbo language, enclitic is a suffix that refers to the meaning of a word preceding it and highlights the word by giving it more emphatic meaning. Enclitic is a morpheme that can either bbe attached to a verb or stand alone in Igbo sentence. In both cases, Igbo enclitic function remains the same i.e. it functions as an extentsion of the meaning of word highlighting on action words.

Enclitic as a spotlight morpheme that brings the verb into a center stage does not render a sentence meaningless when removed from it. Sentences in Igbo language do retain their full meaning without enclictic.

Enclitic can be found in Igbo nouns, pronouns and verbs. When a pronoun precedes an enclitic, the enclitic is written as a standalone but when it is preceded by a verb, the enclitics is attached to the end of the verb to form one word. Examples of Igbo enclitics are: cha, ga, kwa, kwanụ, kwu, nụ, nwa, ri and zi.

1. Anụ cha bụ ihe nwaànyị na-ere n'ahịa.
   Meat <u>in particular</u> is what that woman sells in the market

2. Eze zutara akwụkwọ ga n'ahịa Ogbete.
   Eze bought <u>different</u> books from Ogbete Market.

3. Onye kwa nọ ebe ahụ?
   Who is <u>that person</u> there?

4. Onye kwanụ mebiri ihe osise Eze?
   Who <u>is that person that</u> ruined Eze's painting/drawing?

5. Nri kwu ka O nyeghị Adamma.
   He/she could not <u>even</u> afford to give Adamma food.

6. Achoro m ka I nyere nwaànyị nụ aka.
   I want you to help this <u>particular</u> woman.

7. Ozi nwa erughị Udoka aka.
   That message didn't <u>even</u> get to Udoka.

8. O kwetara ri tupu Ọ mara ihe ọrụ ya bụ.
   He had agreed <u>to the terms</u> before knowing the job duties.

9. Onye zi gwara gi na-emechiri ahia?
   Who <u>is that person that</u> told you that the market is locked.

The above examples show that when an enclitic is preceded by a noun or pronoun, it stands alone as a separate morpheme or word. Other examples as in the above are:

Igbo	English
1. O kwa gi ka m na-agwa?	*Are you not the one I'm talking to?*
2. Unu kwanụ?	*How about you (people/group)?*
3. Mụ nwa gwara ya.	*I personally told him/her.*
4. Mụ kwu?	*... even me?*

5. Anyi zi.   *Every one of us (in particular)*
6. Ha cha   *Every one of them (in particular)*
7. Ha ga   *Every one of them included*
8. Ya sọ   *Him/Her in particular*

In the following sentence examples, we will notice that when an enclitic is preceded by a verb, it is attached to the end of the verb to form one unitary word and still retain its highlighting function. The enclitics affixed to Igbo words are generally in the form of: cha, dị, dụ, fụ, ga, kọ, kwa (kwọ), kwanụ, kwu, nịị, nọọ, nụ, nwa, ra, rị, rịị, tụ, zi, etc.

The most common verbal examples are found in--bịanụ, bụkwa, bụzi, eduga, jicha, jikwu, kpọcha, makwa, matakwanụ, sokwu, etc. For example:

Igbo   English
1. Bianụ hụrụ.   *You (people) should come and see.*
2. Ọ bụkwa nke a ka Ị chọrọ?   *Is this exactly the one you want?*
3. O bụzi ihe ihere.   *It has become a disgrace (shameful).*
4. M ga-eduga ha ụlọ ahịa.   *I will take them to the supermarket.*
5. Ha jicha ụlọ akụ ụgwọ.   *They own the bank some money.*
6. Dinta ahụ jikwu mma.   *That hunter had a machete as well.*
7. Ọ kpọcha gi, Ị bịa hụ m.   *See me, after your (phone) call.*
8. I makwa onye m bụ!   *You do not know exactly who I am.*
9. Matakwanụ na Ọ bụ nkem   *Acknowledge that it belongs to me.*
10. O sokwu agba asịrị   *He/she is one of the gossippers.*

Chapter 18

Allomorphs in Igbo Language
(Ndịiche Mkpụrụasụsụ nke Igbo)

In linguistics, an allomorph is a variant phonetic form of a morpheme, or, a unit of meaning that varies in sound and spelling without changing the meaning. The term allomorph describes the realization of phonological variations for a specific morpheme.

There are many allomorphs in Igbo language due to variant realization of particles, noun agents, noun instruments, infinitives, gerunds, past tense markers, among others. The allomorphs were necessitated due to the grammatical nature of Igbo language following vowel harmony rules besides linguistic restrictions that apply to synonymous words.

There are seven major types of allomorphs in Igbo language, they are:
- *Participles* - Òmekàngwaà
- *Infinitives* - Mfinitiivu
- *Gerund* - Jerọndụ
- *Noun agent* - Ahaome/Omee

Noun instrument - Ahamme/Mmee
Past tense - Nke ihe gara aga
Plural allomorphs - Nke Ụbara

Participles (Òmekàngwaà): A participle is a nonfinite verb form that has some of the characteristics and functions of both verbs and adjectives. Certain groups of people see it as a word derived from a verb and used as an adjective, it is a verbal form of word that needs an auxiliary element to augment its meaning.

In the Igbo language, it is generated by prefixing a corresponding a/e to the verb root in accordance to vowel harmony rules of Igbo language. It is in the form of a/e + verb root = Participle.

Examples with *Participles* (Òmekàngwaà):

Prefix (nganiihu)	**Verb root** (Isingwaa)	**New word** (Mkpụrụokwuọhụru)	**Meaning** (Ihe ọ pụtata)
a	bụ	abụ	*song*
a	da	Ada	*first daughter*
a	kpa	Akpa	*bag*
a	gba	Agba	*jaw*
e	de	Ede	*cocoyam*
e	nyo	Enyo	*mirror*
e	je	Eje	*go (ing)*
e	ti	Eti	*beat (ing)*
a	nwụ	anwụ	*sun*
a	gwụ	agwụ	*maniac*

The 'a' and 'e' of Igbo language are allomorphs because they are different in sound and their spelling is semantically the same. From the example above, you can see that both can be prefixed to the verb root to form infinitives and they are phonological variants of the morpheme. However, they cannot be used interchangeable in the linguistic environment because of Igbo vowel harmony rules.

Furthermore, the infinitive prefixes, 'a' and 'e' can be used as an indefinite pronoun, thus, another form of allomorphs in another grammatical environment. The rule applies here, in all environment where they perform the same grammatical function they cannot be used interchangeably. Examples of 'a' and 'e' as a pronoun is shown below:

Igbo language   *Meaning*
A kụrụ aka.   Someone clapped or knocked (at the door).
E kwuru okwu.   Someone spoke or said something

Infinitives (Mfinitiivu): The *infinitive* is a *grammar* term that refers to a basic verb form that often acts as a noun and is often preceded by the word *to*. An *infinitive* is formed from a verb but doesn't act as a verb. Therefore, one cannot add 's, es, ed, or ing' to the end because it is not a verb. Infinitives can be used as nouns, adjectives or adverbs.

In Igbo language, infinitive is realized by prefixation using the corresponding i/ị prefix in accordance with vowel harmony to any verb root. That is i/ị + verb root = infinitive. It is important to note that these two prefixes are the possible morphemes used in the realization of infinitive in Igbo language.

Examples with infinitives (Mfinitiivu):

Prefix (nganiihu)	Verb root (Isingwaa)	Infinitives (Mfinitiivu)	Meaning (Ihe ọ pụtata)
ị	ba	ịbá	to enter
ị	da	ịda	to fall
ị	kpa	ịkpa	to discuss
ị	gba	ịgba	to play/dane
i	de	ide	to write
i	nyo	enyo	to peek
i	ke	ike (wa)	to divide
ị	ma	ịmá	to know
i	re	irè	to sell
i	zu	izu	to device/steal

The 'i' and 'ị' of Igbo language are allomorphs because they are different in sound and their spelling is semantically the same. From the example above, you can see that both can be prefixed to the verb root to form infinitives and they are phonological variants of the morpheme. However, they cannot be used interchangeable in the linguistic environment because of Igbo vowel harmony rules.

Furthermore, the infinitive prefixes, 'i' and 'ị' can be used as second person singular pronoun, thus, another form of allomorphs in another grammatical environment. The rule applies here, in all environment where they perform the same grammatical function they cannot be used interchangeably. Some examples of 'i' and 'į' as pronouns are shown below:

Igbo language   *Meaning*
I riri nri.   You ate food.
Į ga-eri nri.   You will eat (food).

Gerund (Jerọndụ): A *gerund* is like a blend of verbs and nouns. It looks like a verb, but it acts like a noun. In English ending in -ing. For example, the word swimming, asking looking, talking, playing, etc.

In the Igbo language, gerund is a verbal derivation realized by the prefixing of o/ọ to a reduplicated verb root. It is in the form of O/ọ + verb root x 2 = Gerund.

Examples with *Gerund* (Jerọndụ):

Prefix (nganiihu)	Verb root (Isingwaa)	Infinitives (Mfinitivu)	Gerund (Jerondu)	Meaning (Ihe ọ pụtata)
o	ri	ri	oriri	*eating/feasting*
ọ	nyụ	nya	ọnyụnya	*driving*
ọ	ṅụ	ṅụ	ọṅụṅụ	*drinking*
ọ	dị	da	ọdịda	*falling*
o	di	de	odide	*writing*
ọ	gụ	gụ	ọgụgụ	*reading*
o	ri	re	orire	*selling*
ọ	mụ	mụ	ọmụmụ	*learning/bearing*

ọ	hụ	hụ	ahụhụ	*roasting*
ọ	sụ	sọ	ọsụsọ	*sweating*
o	bi	bi	obibi	*living (home)*
o	ti	ti	otiti	*beating*

The 'o' and 'ọ' of Igbo language are allomorphs because they are different in sound and their spelling is semantically the same. From the example above, you can see that both can be prefixed to the verb root to form infinitives and they are phonological variants of the morpheme. However, they cannot be used interchangeable in the linguistic environment because of Igbo vowel harmony rules.

Furthermore, the infinitive prefixes, 'o' and 'ọ' can be used as third person singular pronoun, thus, another form of allomorphs in another grammatical environment. The rule applies here; in all environments where they perform the same grammatical function they cannot be used interchangeably. Examples of 'o' and 'ọ' as a pronoun is shown below:

Igbo language   *Meaning*
O dere ihe.   S/he wrote something.
Ọ gara ahịa.   S/he went to the market.

Noun agent (Ahaomee/Omee): an agent noun is a word that is derived from another word denoting an action, and that identifies an entity that does that action. For example, "driver" is an agent noun formed from the verb "drive". Most agent nouns end in either '-er' (standard) or '-or' in the English language (for words derived directly from Latin e.g. carpenter, debtor, electrician, employer, lecturer, performer, director, teacher, etc.

In the Igbo language, the agent noun is realized by the use of the prefix o/ọ to the verb root and the addition of a noun complement.
o/ọ + verb root + Noun complement = Agent Noun

Example with Noun agent (Ahaomee/Omee):

Prefix (nganiihu)	*Two verb root* (Isingwaa abụọ)	*Noun Agent* (Ahaomee/Omee)	*Meaning* (Ihe ọ pụtata)
o	me + e	Omee	*(noun) agent*
o	de + e	Ode	*writer*
o	le + e	Olee	*where/how many*
o	me + e	Omee	*doer*
ọ	ga + a	ọgaa	*boss*
ọ	gba + a	ọgbaa	*shooter*
ọ	kụ + ụ	ọkụụ	*planter/sower*
ọ	sụ + ụ	ọsụụ	*speaker/cutter*
ọ	ṅụ + ụ	ọṅụụ	*drinker*
o	je + e	Ojee	*traveler/goer*

Noun instrument (Ahammee/Mmee): Instrument noun: it is the equipment a worker uses in carrying out his duty. In the Igbo language, noun instrument is obtained when an m/n are prefixed to the verb root and the addition of a noun complement. The combination is in the following form:
m/n + verb root + Noun complement = Instrument Noun

Example with Noun instrument (Ahammee/Mmee):

Prefix (nganiihu)	Verb root (Isingwaa)	Complement (Mmeju)	Ahamme/Mmee (Noun Instrument)	Translation (Ntụgharị)
m	gba	mmiri	mgbammiri	*jug*
m	pa	naka	mpanaka	*hand lamp*
m	kpa	isi	mkpaisi	*scissors*
m	gba	ama	mgbaama	*revealer*
n	che	ndo	nchendo	*sun protector*
n	ti	mkpu	nti mkpu	*exclaimer*
n	ku	ikuku	nku ikuku	*fan*
n	de	akwa	nde akwa	*iron*
n	tụ	oyi	ntụ oyi	*air conditioner*
n	gụ	ọnụ	ngụ ọnụ	*counter*

Past tense (Nke ihe gara aga): *past tense* is the verb form you use to talk about things that happened in the past. Past tense indicates that an action is in the past relative to the speaker or writer. It is the use of verb to express an event that happened that is being talked about or reported.

In English, we use the past tense morpheme "ed", which is most often used with past regular verbs, for example: "planted", or "washed". It always has the same function (of making a verb past), but is pronounced slightly differently depending on the verb it is bound to: in "washed" we get /t/ (wash/t/), and in "planted" we get /ɪd/ (plant /ɪd/).

In the Igbo language, the letter "r" combines with any of the letters of Igbo vowels to produce an expression in the past tense. For example:

Verb root	/r/	Vowel	Past tense	meaning
fọ	r	ọ	fọrọ	remained
ga	r	a	gara	went
kwu	r	u	kwuru	said
re	r	e	rere	sold
ri	r	i	riri	ate
sị	r	ị	sịrị	said
tụ	r	ụ	tụrụ	threw
zo	r	o	zoro	hid

Therefore, -ra, -re, -ri, -rị, -ro, -rọ, -ru, -rụ are allomorphs in the above examples and they denote past tense of the verb root. They follow vowel harmony rules during combination. For example, you cannot put forward the following : *forọ, *gare, *kwurụ, *reri, *rirụ,
*siro, *tụra and *zori,

Plural (Nke Ụbara): Plural is one of the values of the grammatical category of number. The plural of a noun typically denotes a quantity greater than the default quantity represented by that noun. Plural markers are affixes or letters added to singular nouns to make them plural. Once a plural marker is added to a singular noun, that noun becomes countable. The plural markers of English are: 's,' 'es,' 'ves' and 'ies' as in 'boy - boys', 'church - churches', 'thief - thieves' and 'lady - ladies', etc.

In the Igbo language plural markers are a form of allomorphs. The plural markers in the Igbo language are 'ndị' and 'ụmụ'. They increase the value or number of a noun element and make them to become more than one element. Like other allomorphs, they are not interchangeable in an environment. For example:

Singular	Meaning	Plural	Meaning
Nwa akwụkwọ	a student	ụmụ akwụkwọ	Students
Nwa nne	a sibling	ụmụ nne	Siblings
Nwa nnụnụ	a bird	ụmụ nnụnụ	birds

In the above examples, although 'ụmụ' and 'ndị' are both plural markers as well as allomorph, they cannot be interchanged in the above context due to connotational restriction. When used in the above context, it becomes an expression of mockery to the person or group in question. 'ndị akwụkwọ' can suggest derogatory or belittling comment.

The use of the "ndị" plural marker is in the right context in the following examples:

Singular	Meaning	Plural	Meaning
Onye nne	a mother	ndị nne	mothers
Onye nna	a father	ndị nna	fathers

'Ụmụ' and 'ndị' are allomorphs. They connote plural but their forms are different and they operate under specific and selective linguistic environment due to some restriction that applies to them contextually, connotatively or collocationally.

Part Four:

Lexicology in Igbo Linguistics (Amụmàmụ Ụdịdị, Nghọta na Itinye Mkpụrụokwu Igbo N'ọrụ)

Chapter 19

Introduction to Lexicology (Mmalite Amụmàmụ Nghọta Mkpụrụokwu)

What is Lexicology?
Lexicology is the branch of linguistics that is concerned with the study of words as individual items. It deals with both formal and semantic aspects of words; and analyzes the vocabulary of a specific language. Although, it is concerned predominantly with an in-depth description of lexemes, it gives a close attention to a vocabulary in its totality, the social communicative essence of a language as a synergetic system being a study focus. Lexicology examines every feature of a word – including formation, spelling, origin, usage and definition. It also considers the relationships that exist between words.

In linguistics, the lexicon (vocabulary) of a language is composed of lexemes, which are abstract units of meaning that correspond to a set of related forms of a word. Lexicology looks at how words can be broken down as well as identifies common patterns they follow. Lexicology is associated with lexicography, which is the practice of compiling dictionaries.

As every word is a unity of semantic, phonetic and grammatical elements, the word is studied not only in lexicology, but in other branches of linguistics, too, lexicology being closely connected with general linguistics, the history of the language, phonetics, stylistics, and grammar.

Lexicology interrelation with other branches of linguistics:
Lexicology (from Gr *lexis* "word" and logos "learning") is a part of linguistics dealing with the vocabulary of a language and the properties of words as the main units of the language. It also studies all kinds of semantic grouping and semantic relations: synonym, antonym, hyponymy, semantic fields, etc.

In this connection, the term vocabulary is used to denote a system formed by the sum total of all the words and word equivalents that the language possesses. The term word denotes the basic unit of a given language resulting from the association of a particular meaning with a particular group of sounds capable of a particular grammatical employment. A word therefore is at the same time a semantic, grammatical and phonological unit. So, the subject-matter of lexicology is the word, its morphemic structure, history and meaning. Vocabulary studies include such aspects of research as etymology, semasiology and onomasiology.

Etymology: The evolution of a vocabulary forms the object of historical lexicology or etymology (from Gr. *etymon* "true, real"), discussing the origin of various words, their change and development, examining the linguistic and extra-linguistic forces that modify their structure, meaning and usage.

Semasiology (from Gr. *semasia* "signification") is a branch of linguistics whose subject-matter is the study of word meaning and the classification of changes in the signification of words or forms, viewed as normal and vital factors of any linguistic development. It is the most relevant to polysemy and homonymy.

Onomasiology is the study of the principles and regularities of the signification of things / notions by lexical and lexico-phraseological means of a given language. It has its special value in studying dialects, bearing an obvious relevance to synonymity.

What is lexicography?
Lexicology is the science of the study of word whereas lexicography is the writing of the word in some concrete form i.e. in the form of dictionary. As we shall see later, lexicology and lexicography are very closely related, rather the latter is directly dependent on the former and may be called applied lexicology.

Lexicography, the oldest sub-discipline of linguistics, deals with the compilation of dictionaries. There are many types of dictionaries, depending mainly on which lexical units are included, and which of their properties—such as sound, spelling, grammatical features, meaning, etymology, and others—are described.

One further important objective of lexicological studies is the study of the vocabulary of a language as a system. Revising the issue, the vocabulary can be studied synchronically (at a given stage of its development), or diachronically (in the context of the processes through which it grew, developed and acquired its modern form). The opposition of the two approaches is nevertheless disputable as the vocabulary, as well as the word which is its fundamental unit, is not only what it is at this particular stage of the language development, but what it was centuries ago and has been throughout its history.

The concept of Lexeme:
The term lexeme means a language's most basic unit of meaning, often also thought of as a word in its most basic form. Not all lexemes consist of just one word, though, as a combination of words are necessary to convey the intended meaning. Examples of lexemes include walk, fire station, and change of heart. Lexeme can be defined to include this and these in one lexeme, or as two. Demonstratives like this have little or no lexical meaning, which is the point of "lexemes". Run is a lexeme in runner, running, runs, ran because they have related meanings; this has no meaning at all outside a deictic context.

A lexeme is (i) a lexical abstraction that (ii) has either a meaning (ordinarily) or a grammatical function, (iii) belongs to a syntactic category (most often a lexical category), and (iv) is realized by one or more phonological forms (canonically, by morphosyntactically contrasting word forms).

The study of lexeme in relation to word form
There are three lower levels of a language – a phoneme, a morpheme, a word. A word is the smallest meaningful unit of a language that can stand on its own, and is made up of small components called morphemes and even smaller elements known

as phonemes, or distinguishing sounds. Being a central element of any language system, the word is a focus for the problems of phonology, lexicology, syntax, morphology, stylistics and also for a number of other language and speech sciences.

The modern approach to the word as a double-facet unit is based on distinguishing between *the external* and *the internal structures of the word*. By the *external structure* of the word we mean *its morphological structure*. For example, in the word *post-impressionists* the following morphemes can be distinguished: the prefixes *post-*, *im-*, the root *–press-*, the noun-forming suffixes *-ion*, *-ist*, and the grammatical suffix of plurality *-s*. All these morphemes constitute the external structure of the word *post-impressionists*. *The internal structure of the word*, or *its meaning*, is nowadays commonly referred to as **the word's semantic structure**. This is the word's main aspect. Words can serve the purpose of human communication solely due to their meanings.

To sum it up, a word is the smallest naming unit of a language with a more or less free distribution used for the purposes of human communication, materially representing a group of sounds, possessing a meaning, susceptible to grammatical employment and characterized by formal and semantic unity.

There are **4 basic kinds of words:**
1) Orthographic words – this refers to words distinguished from each other by their spelling. Orthography is the part of language study concerned with letters and spelling. It is the art of writing words with the proper letters, according to accepted usage; correct spelling. This method of spelling, is by the use of an alphabet or other system of symbols.

2) **Phonological words** – distinguished from each other by their pronunciation, the phonological word or prosodic word is a constituent in the phonological hierarchy higher than the syllable and the foot but lower than intonational phrase and the phonological phrase. Phonological words may be smaller or larger than grammatical or orthographic words.

It is difficult to find single and fixed criteria, which can be used to define a unit 'phonological word' in every language. There is a range of types of criteria such that every language, which has a unit 'phonological word', uses a selection of these criteria. The criteria include: segmental features, suprasegmental (prosodic) and phonological rules.

A phonological word can be realized depending on the different segmental features of a word. For example; sequence of phoneme types, vowel clusters between consecutive syllable, possible positioning of phonemes within a word, role of aspiration and nasalization and pausal phenomena etc. Vowel clusters occur in words with adjoining vowels. These vowel combinations are associated with specific sounds. For example, the "ee" spelling denotes a long "e" sound, as in "Ee." (translated as "yes" in English), the position of phonemes within a word involves the conditions in which phonemes are realized in speech.

Stress (or accent) and/ or tone assignment; prosodic (suprasegmental) features such as nasalization, retroflexion, vowel harmony. Stress or accent, in many languages proves one helpful criterion for defining a phonological word. It becomes easier to find the position of word boundaries from the location of stress in a word, but in some languages, stress placement may depend on a combination of morphological and phonological factors. In such cases, stress may not be a useful criterion for phonological word. A phonological word can be realized in terms of vowel harmony, which operates over a certain syntagmatic extent (see chapter two). Vowel harmony may constitute a necessary and sufficient condition for recognizing a phonological word but not all languages have such convenient phonetic rules, and even those that do present the occasional exceptions.

3) **Word-forms** which are grammatical variants; are the different ways a word can exist in the context of a language. Many words exist as nouns, verbs or adjectives and change when prefixes or suffixes are added. For example, in English language, the words beautify, beautiful and beautifully are the verb, adjective and adverb forms of the noun beauty, but they are not interchangeable when used in a sentence.

Here are some word forms:

Noun	*Verb*	*Adjective*	*Adverb*
Beauty	beautify	beautiful	beautifully
Beneficiary	benefit	beneficial	beneficially
Creation	create	creative	creatively
Decision	decide	decisive	decisively
Difference	differentiate	different	differently

4) Words as items of meaning, the headwords of dictionary entries, are called **lexemes**. **A lexeme** is a group of words united by the common lexical meaning, but having different grammatical forms. The base forms of such words, represented either by one

orthographic word or a sequence of words called **multi-word lexemes** which have to be considered as single lexemes (e.g. phrasal verbs, some compounds) may be termed **citation forms of lexemes** (sing, talk, head, etc.), from which other word forms are considered to be derived.

Any language is a system of systems consisting of two subsystems: 1) the system of words' possible lexical meanings; 2) the system of words' grammatical forms. The former is called **the semantic structure of the word**; the latter is **its paradigm** latent to every part of speech (e.g. a noun has a 4-member paradigm, an adjective – a 3-member paradigm, etc.)

As for **the main lexicological problems**, two of these have already been highlighted. The problem of word-building is associated with prevailing morphological word-structures and with the processes of coining new words. Semantics is the study of meaning. Modern approaches to this problem are characterized by two different levels of study: syntagmatic and paradigmatic.

On the **syntagmatic level**, the semantic structure of the word is analyzed in its linear relationships with neighboring words in connected speech. In other words, the semantic characteristics of the word are observed, described and studied on the basis of its typical contexts.

On the **paradigmatic level**, the word is studied in its relationships with other words in the vocabulary system. So, a word may be studied in comparison with other words of a similar meaning (e. g. *work*, n. – *labor*, n.; *to refuse*, v. – *to reject* v. – to *decline*, v.), of opposite meaning (e. g. *busy*, adj. – *idle*, adj.; *to accept*, v. – *to* *reject*, v.), of different stylistic characteristics (e. g. *man*, n. – *chap*, n. – *bloke*, n. — *guy*, n.). Consequently, the key problems of paradigmatic studies are synonymy, antonymy, and functional styles.

Chapter 20

Word Building (Word Formation) (Usoro Mmụba Okwu Igbo)

Word Formation Process is a means by which new words are produced either by modification of existing words or by complete innovation, which in turn become a part of the language. A morpheme is the smallest element of a word or else a grammar element, whereas a word is a complete meaningful element of language.

A word is a unit of language that carries meaning and consists of one or more morphemes which are joined more or less tightly together. A word consists of a root or stem and/or more affixes. Words can be combined to create phrases, clauses, and sentences. The study of the origin and history of a word is known as word etymology, a term which comes from Latin, but has its origins in Greek as (e´tymon "originalform" + logia "study of").

In Igbo language, most formed words are usually independent of complement. However, if the new word is a noun, it would have its complements attached. Examples:

word	meaning	class	new word	meaning	class
ozi	(message)	noun	oga ozi	messenger	noun
ri	(eat)	verb-	o-ri nri	(eater)	noun
ti	(drum)	verb	o-ti igba	(drummer)	noun

In the previous chapter, we learned that morphological process in Igbo language can be divided into seven formal and three methods. The formal kinds of Igbo word formation are: Affixation, Clipping, Compounding, Borrowing/Loanword, Reduplication, Blending and Acronyms. We had an indepth study on affixation as one of the seven kinds of word formation or morphological process.

The three informal methods are: Jests/slangs (Njakịrị/Akụkụ), Mispronounced/corrupt words (Okwu Mkpọhie) and Loan blend words (Mbiọgwa).

In this chapter, we will focus on Clipping, Compounding, Borrowing/Loanword, Reduplication, Blending and Acronyms with their appropriate examples for better understanding.

Clipping
Clipping is the process of forming a new word by dropping one or more syllables from a polysyllabic word. it is the shortening of polysyllabic words without regard to derivation. This reduction process becomes possible because of a single syllable usually the one bearing the main stress. A common example in English is the forming of cellphone from cellular phone. Other examples are: ad for advertisement and phone for telephone.

The term clipping is also known as a clipped form, clipped word, shortening, and truncation. Words are clipped when they are in a closely restricted context which leads to dropping the redundant syllables.

There are four types of possible clipping processes, depending on which part of the word undergoes structural changes. The four types of clipping are: back-clipping, fore-clipping, mixed clipping and clipping compunds. The examples in English are:

1. Back-clipping: temperature as temp, rhinoceros as rhino, gymnasium as gym, cellular as cell, etc.
2. Fore-clipping: helicopter as copter, telephone as phone, aeroplane as plane.
3. Mixed clipping: influenza as flu, refrigerator as fridge.
4. Clipping-compounds: parachute + trooper as paratrooper.

In Igbo language, the first two types are predominant in Igbo names and other noun or noun phrase.

Examples of back-clipping in Igbo words:

Word	*Clipped form*	*Full meaning*
Amaobichukwu	Amobi	*God's heart is unsearchable*
Arụrụ ala	Aru	*evil act or abominable act*
Chibụeze	Chibu	*God is king*
Chimaramkpam	Chi'ma	*God knows my need*
Chimdinma	Chidi	*my God is good*
Chimsomaga	Chisom	*My God is with me*
Chinụalamọgụ	Chinua	*may God fight for me*

Ginikanwa	Ginika	*what is bigger than a child?*
nkemdịrịm	Nkem	*let my portion be for me*
Nwakaego	Nwa'ka	*Child surpasses money*
Obịoha	Obi	*people's dearness*
Ogechukwu	Oge	*God's time*
Uzọchukwuamaka	Ụzọchukwu	*God's way is beautiful*

Examples of fore-clipping in Igbo words:

Word	Clipped form	Full meaning
Chinọnye	Nọnye	*(may) God stays with me*
Ndụmọdụ	Ọdụ	*advice*
Nwaamaka	Amaka	*(to have) baby is beautiful*
Ọgba-aghara	Aghara	*confusion*
Onye isi	Isi	*head*
Onyebụchi	Bụchi	*who is equal to God?*
Onyekachi	Kachi	*Who is bigger than God*
Ukwuosisi	Osisi	*tree*
Umengwu	Ngwu	*weakness*

Compounding

Compounding is the morphological operation that puts together two free forms and gives rise to a new word. In this process, new words are formed or derived by combining stems or root morphemes. For example, in English language, if you take the free morpheme white, an adjective, and combine it with the free morpheme house, a noun, I get the new word whitehouse.

In compounding the two words or morphemes that are used to form a new word usually have equal morphological status. This process of joining together of different lexical items to form new words does not necessarily require the change of class of the words.

Compounding	New word	Translation
Di +mgba	Dimgba	wrester
Elu + igwe	Eluigwe	heaven
Isi+ akwukwo	isiakwukwo	brainy
M + kpa + isi	Mkpaisi	scissors
N + kọwa + okwu	Nkọwaokwu	dictionary
N + ti + igba	Ntiigba	drum stick
Ndi+ oshi	Ndioshi	thieves
Nwa+ akwụkwọ	nwaakwụkwọ	student/pupil
Ọ + kọwa + okwu	Ọkọwaokwu	lexicographer
Ọ + kpụ + isi	Ọkpụisi	barber
O + ti + igba	Otiigba	drummer
Odee + akwụkwọ	odeakwụkwọ	secretary
Oje + mba	Ojemba	Tourist
Onye+ nkuzi	onyenkuzi	teacher
Oshi+ ite	Oshite	cook
Ụgbọ + ala	Ụgbọala	car
Ụgbọ + elu	Ụgbọelu	airplane
Ulo + akwukwo	Ụlọakwụkwọ	school

Coined Words (Okwu Apịrịapị)

Coined words are new words invented or made up through the joining of two or more existing words. Coined words are similar to word formation through compounding except for the fact that the new word may modify any part of the words for easy pronunciation and to distinguish it from phrasal expression. Coined words are formed using either the features or functions of a thing. Popular use of a coined word is what makes it an acceptable part of Igbo word.

For example:

Coined word	Translation	Meaning/Usage
Ahịa enwemenwe	*ownable market*	Stock market
Akpatịokwu okwu	*Talkative box*	Radio
Akpatịokwu	*Chattering box*	Radio
Akụ enwemenwe	*ownable Wealth*	Stock
Asambodo	*Asambodo*	Certificate
Ekwentị	*Ear Gong*	Handset
Igwe okwu okwu	*metal for speakers*	Microphone
Igwe okwu	*metal for talking*	Microphone
Mahadum	*know it all*	University
Mgboojii/mgbo odee	*Blackboard*	Blackboard
Mkpịsị odee	*writer's pen/pencil*	Pen, pencil
Nnyemeakangwaa	*Auxiliary verb*	Auxiliary verb
Ntorobịa	*young (man/woman)*	Youths
Ntụli aka	*to put up hand*	Vote
Nzere	*Defense (of project)*	Degree
Nzu odee	*writer's chalk*	Chalk
Ọba akwụkwọ	*book barn*	Library
Ọchịchị ndị agbada	*civilian rule*	civilian rule
Ọgbọ nta vootu	*voter's specified area*	Constitutency
Ogbunigwe	*kills in multitude*	Bomb
Ọkada	*loud noise (bike)*	Motocycle
Oke ọnwụnye	*earnable part/share*	Share
Okooko	*Flower*	Flower
Onyoonyo	*item for viewing*	Television
Ọrịa mmịnwụ	*shrinking illness*	HIV/AIDS

Ọrịa obilinaajaọcha	*grave destined illness*	HIV/AIDS
Ọzutaakụ	*Wealth buyer*	Stock broker
Ụgbọ okporoigwe	*metal track vehicle*	Train
Ụka ọgbaraọhụrụ	*Modern day's church*	Pentecostal church
Ụkọ akwụkwọ	*book holder/hanger*	Bookshelf
Ụzọ awaraawara	*graded/broad way*	Express road

The above listed coined words are used either to describe a feature or function thereby forming a noun that are used for system or things that are new in Igbo language. Notice that coined words can have up to six or more words in order to give full meaning and make the description easy to understand. For example:

Coined word	Translation	No. of words
Ndị ejị okwu ha eme ihe	*Stake-holders*	6
Nnweghari enwe+m+enwe	*Stock exchange*	4
Ọchịchị+onye kwuo uche ya	*Demoncracy*	5

Borrowed/Loan Word
Borrowing is the process by which a word from one language is adapted for use in another. Words from source language are borrowed or loaned as lexical items to another language. All languages are susceptible to borrowing for lexical expansion so as to cope with new functions and to meet up with their limited names for things they have no name for.

Also, borrowing can result from trade and commerce especially where language association or linguistic contact among languages meet. Borrowing is perhaps the most common source of new words and should be seen as a regular morphological process of word formation in every language. Borrowed words are called loanwords.

Examples of Igbo loan words:

Loan word	Source	Translation
Adure	Yoruba	*dyed cloth from yoruba*
Agbada	Yoruba	*traditional free flowing outfit*
Agboro	Hausa	*tout*
Agidi	Yoruba	*solid cooked pap*
Ahụekere	Hausa	*goundnut*
Akamụ	Hausa	*Pap*
Akpati	Yoruba	*box*
Alafịa	Hausa	*enjoyment*
Alịbọ	Ịgala	*powdered cassava*
Ashawo	Yoruba	*Harlot*
Ashebi	Yoruba	*uniform attire in ceremony*
Asioke	Yoruba	*locally weaved cloth*
Ayo	Yoruba	*onions*
Banza	Hausa	*rubbish*
Bọl/bọọlụ	English	*Ball*
Bredị	English	*Bread*
Burukutu	Hausa	*fermented drink*
Chịnchị	Hausa	*bedbug*
Dada	Yoruba	*dreadlock*
Disemba	English	*December*
Ekpeteshi	Ghana	*Rum*
Ekpo	Calabar/Ibibio	*type of masquered*
Eba	Yoruba	*Garri meal*
Faksi	English	*Fax*
Friza	English	*Freezer*
Gova	Portuguese	*Guava*

Gworo	Hausa	*type of kola*
Ịchafo	Hausa	*headtie/Scarf*
Ịntanet	English	*Internet*
Isam	Ịjaw/Efik	*periwinkle (snail)*
Jara	Hausa	*add small/extra*
Jenuwari	English	*January*
Jigida	Hausa	*type of waist bead*
Kaikai	Yoruba	*locally distilled liquor*
Kanda	Hausa	*used as meat or grilled meat*
Karọtụ	English	*Carrot*
Kashu	Portuguese	*Cashew*
Kebụlụ	English	*cable*
Koboko	Hausa	*whip*
Kọmputa	English	*computer*
Kpekele	Yoruba	*fried dried plantain*
Maịmaị/Elele	Yoruba	*prepared beans meal/cake*
Mangala	Hausa	*Fish (a type of fish)*
Mango	English	*Mango*
Mọị-mọị	Yoruba	*beans cake/meal*
Mọnde	English	*Monday*
Moto	English	*motor*
Mugu	onye nzuuzu	*a gullible/foolish person*
Netwọkụ	English	*network*
Njin	English	*engine*
Njinịa	English	*engineer*
Ọga	Yoruba	*master*
Ogede	Ịgala	*plantain*
Okwute	Yoruba	*stone*
Onuku/Oluku	Ịgala	*idiot/fool*
Osikapa	Hausa	*rice*
Oyooyo	Yoruba	*delicious*

Pọọpọ	English	*pawpaw*
Redio	English	*radio*
Salaka	Chad/Yoruba	*generous/free gift*
Suya	Hausa	*peppery smoked meat*
Tebulu	English	*table*
Tọọchi	English	*torch*
Tozo	Hausa	*cow's rhomboid muscles*
Trauza	English	*trouser*
Tuuzdee	English	*tuesday*
Vidio	English	*video*
Wahala	Yoruba	*trouble*
Waka	Hausa	*abuse*
Waya	English	*wire*
Wayo	Yoruba	*cheat*
Windo	English	*window*
Wuruwuru	Yoruba	*deception/cheating*
Yabasi	Hausa	*onion*

The borrowed word never remains a perfect copy of its original. It is made to fit the phonological, morphological, and syntactic patterns of its new language. For example, the Hausa pronunciation of shinkafa is very different from the Igbo pronunciation Osikapa. Likewise, the Hausa pronunciation of albasa is pronounce Yabasi in Igbo language. The same applies to so many other borrowed words.

Reduplication
Reduplication is a morphological process in which the root or stem of a word or even the whole word is repeated exactly or with a slight change. Reduplication is common in Igbo language. It is also, a word-formation process in which all or part of a word is

repeated to convey some form of meaning.

Reduplication is often used to show plurality, distribution, repetition, customary activity, increase of size, added intensity, continuance, etc. It is found in many languages of the world, however, its morphological methods vary from language to language.

In general, reduplication is a process of repeating a syllable or the word as a whole (sometimes with a vowel change) and putting it together to form a new word. In English language words like byebye (exact reduplication), super-duper (rhyming reduplication) or chitchat, pitter-patter, zigzag, tick-tock, ,flipflop are examples of reduplication.

Examples of reduplication Igbo words:

Two similar Words	*Reduplicated form*	*Translation*
Aga + aga	Agaaga	*impassable*
Aja + aja	Ajaaja	sandy
Aka + aka	Akaaka	ageless/timeless
Aṅwụ + aṅwụ	Aṅwụaṅwụ	immortal/deathless
Anya + anya	Anyaanya	looker/staring
Ata + ata	Ataata	sinewy
Awa + awa	Awaawa	unbreakable
Eri + eri	Erieri	stingy
Mkpu + mkpu	mkpumkpu	shortness
Mmiri + mmiri	Mmiri mmiri	watery
Ngwa + ngwa	Ngwangwa	hurriedly
Ngwọ + ngwọ	Ngwọngwọ	pepper soup
Ọsọ + ọsọ	Ọsọsọ	hurriedly

Blending

Blending is a morphological process of taking two or more mrophemes or words, removing parts of each, and joining the residues together to create a new word whose form and meaning are taken from the source words. It is typically accomplished by taking only the beginning of one word and joining it to the end of the other word.

In Igbo words formation, if there are two vowels in each of those separate morphemes, one of such vowels is dropped before the new word is realized. For instance, anya + anwụ becomes anyanwụ (sunshine), a is dropped. See more examples below:

Blending	*New word*	*Translation*
anya + anwụ	anyanwụ	sunshine
chi + na + asa	chinasa	God answers
chi +na + eke	chineke	God the creator
Di + ibia	dibia	doctor
di+ ike	dike	strong
nwa + oke	nwoke	male/man
nwa + orie	nworie	child born on orie day
nwa+ afọ	nwafọ	child born on afọ day
nwa+ eke	nweke	child born on eke day
uka + amaka	ukamaka	Church/way (going) is good
uso + ekwu	usekwu	stove/tripod wood stove

Acronyms

Acronym is formed by joining together the initial letters (or sometimes a little larger parts of other words and is pronounced as a word. It is important to note that acronym is not the same thing as abbreviation.

Abbreviation is the shortening of existing words to create a new word, usually in a form that is informal to the originals. There are several ways this can be done. It includes making one or more syllables shorter leaving out other, as in doc for document, Dr. for doctor, app for application and prof for professor. Usually the syllable remaining after the rest has been removed provides enough information to allow us to identify the word it is an abbreviation of, though at times this is not the case.

The difference between acronym and an abbreviation is that abbreviation is usually formed shortening, e.g. doc, dr, prof and so on, while acronyms is formed from the letter of each word.

In some instances the acronym is pronounced as a sequence of letter names, as in UN, US, or SUV. In other instances, such as WHO from World Health Organization and UNICEF from United Nations International Children's Emergency Fund, the acronym can be pronounced as an ordinary English word.

There are few acronyms in Igbo language. This may be because Igbo language and culture embrace comprehensive expression of message in words or they use figure of speech to populate a message which demands deep mental thought and reasoning from the listeners. Some of the common Igbo language acronyms are as follows:

Acronuym	*Full expression*	*Translation*
DGZ	dere gawazie	etcetera/and so on

ONU	Onye Nche Uka	Church warden
ONI	Ome N' ala Igbo	Igbo customs and traditions

INFORMAL WORD FORMATION METHODS

Slang/Jests (Njakịrị/Akụkụ)
Slang is often considered as very informal words and expressions that are more common in speech than writing, and are typically restricted to a particular context or group of people. A set of colloquial words or phrases in a language.
Slang is very colloquial; the language and dialect tend to be specific to a particular territory and it is considered as "youth language" by many adults.

Though, certain jests and slangs are typically restricted to a particular context or group of people, it is language and culture specific and is often transmitted from one culture and language to another. With the advent of internet and mobile communications, the rate at which slangs or jests are being used and shared on social media has increased.

There are several forms of Igbo language jests and slangs but there are seven major categories that they can fall under, namely:
1. *Advisory words* (okwu ndụmọdụ)
2. *Assaultive jest/slang* (okwu mkparị)
3. *Disgraceful words* (okwu mmebọ)
4. *Flaring words* (okwu njali)
5. *Hypercritical jest/slang* (okwu akọmụọnụ)
6. *Laudatory words* (okwu otito)
7. *Side-talk* (okwu akụkụ)

Jests and slangs usually start from either a location or group of people. When it starts from a location or group and becomes common in that location or among the group, it will inadvertently find its way into the society where people can choose to localize it or use it without restriction. The location or group of people could be students, traders, construction workers, young men and women, musicians, media or journalists, broadcasters, and so on.

When a jest or slang is formed and used for the first time, it is usually the people around at the time that would have full understanding of the meaning and it is through them that the meaning and intention is conveyed to other people that would hear the jest or slang later. Hence, when it becomes common to everyone; it would then become a new word. If it is not considered as a derogatory or hate phrase, many people would start using it.

Situational/Advisory words (**okwu ọnọdụ/ndụmọdụ**): these are words that are used to describe a thing, a situation, condition of thing, behavior and lifestyle. They may come in the form of advisory or coded situational expression. Some of the jests/slang may come in the form of a noun, phrase, clause, figure of speech, and so on. For example:

Igbo word	*English translation*
Aghọtaghị ije	*Unable to understand what is going on*
Anịkịrịja	*An old bicycle that makes a lot of noise*
Bọchaa	*Escape/Get out immediately*
Bredị	*Money*
Gbachaa m	*Give me money or find something for me*
Ịghọta ije	*Able to understand what is going on*
Ịnya mmadụ	*To trick somebody*

Na-ekwe oyooyo	*Affirmation/acclamation for looking good*
Oko	*An old person*
Okongwu	*An old person*
Owu ịsa mmadụ	*Serious lack of money*
Owu ite	*bankrupt/poverty-stricken*
Paakuul	*Cool down/relax*
Sụlịa	*To play football well*
Ụwa mgbede	*prosperity towards the end of one's life*
Wụsa ọwara	*To ask someone calm down or relax*

Assaultive jest/slang (**okwu mkparị**): is a word that shows gross indignity, an instance of insolent or contemptuous word or speech that is used to describe an action, behavior and lifestyle. Some of the jests/slang may come in the form of noun, phrase, clause, figure of speech, and so on. For example:

Igbo word	*English translation*
Akụla	*Madness*
Atịmgbo/atịlarị	*A deaf person*
Mugu	*A novice or person who is not sociable*
Mumu	*Foolishness*
Okpo	*A foolish person/A stupid person*
Onye mgbu	*A foolish/stupid person*
Onye owo	*A loser*
Ọnyụpa	*Slow/sluguish movement*

Disgraceful words (**okwu mmebọ**): is a word that brings a deserving loss of reputation or respect as the result of a dishonorable action. It is a shameful, dishonorable and disreputable expression that tells that someone has been exposed for his or her shameful act. Some of the jests/slang may come in the form of noun, phrase, clause, figure of speech, and so on. For example:

Igbo word	English translation
Gbara ọgwụ gị nwụọ	Mind your business
Ịgba buutu	To ignore somebody
Ịkụpụ ntị	To ignore
Ilita mmadụ	To avoid somebody politely
Itebọ/imebọ mmadụ	To disgrace somebody
Ịwụ n'ala	To humiliate somebody
O chogo gị	You have missed something

Flaring words (okwu njali): is a word that brings a deserving motivation or flares up someone's reputation or flashy name. It is a boastful and exaggerated expression that tells about someone status, a magnified status or exaggerated action. Some of the jests/slang may come in the form of noun, phrase, clause, figure of speech, and so on. For example:

Igbo word	English translation
Akpụrụka	Well-built/strong (though not original)
Awara awara	Fast running vehicle
Gbaraagba	A huge person
Ịkpa ọwa	To drive a motocycle/vehicle meticulously
Kụsuo/pịasuo	To provoke/ ginger somebody to act
Obere nsị	A stout-hearted person
Onye ọwa	A person who drives meticulously
Waa waa wa	Wreckless driving

Hypercritical jest/slang **(okwu akọmụọnụ):** is a word that is excessively and unreasonably critical of someone's behaviour, (sometimes of small faults). It may not come as a result of unnecessary faultfinding but a different choice of words that describes someone inadequacy, immaturity or intentional misbehaviour. Some of the jests/slang may come in the form a noun, phrase, clause, figure of speech and so on. For example:

Igbo word	English translation
Anịnị	*A thief/Robber*
Ipara	*Attempt to pay less for more value (product)*
Ịparaala/ịparaana	*Stingy buyer*
JJC	*Newcomer/Fresher*
Mpịrịmpị	*A staunch bargainer*
Nzama	*Cheating with profit*
Ogbu oge (abbr. "oo")	*Someone who wastes precious time*
Ọta mgbe	*Someone who wastes his precious time*

Laudatory words **(okwu otito):** are words that express praise; extolling someone or something. It is a eulogistic or commendatory expression that can be used to describe the specialty or uniqueness of a thing or someone. It may come in the form of flattery words or sincere words of admiration of someone action, personality or beauty. Some of the jests/slang may come in the form of noun, phrase, clause, figure of speech and so on. For example:

Igbo word	English translation
Ajịbọ	*elegant or sophisticated lady*
Aka nchawa	*Good luck*
Akwa nwa	*A pretty woman/lady/baby*

Asụkaramụ	*Richness/wealth*
Bebi ị dị okee	*A pretty lady who dresses very beautiful*
Ebe anọ	*Current trend*
Ị chara ife ị ga-acha	*You are looking good*
I nwerọ polo	*You don't have any problem*
Ị towara ntị	*very beautiful/dressing very beautiful*
Ichi okere	*To show off*
Igbu ozu	*Richness/wealth*
Iji ija	*Richness*
Iji nkụ	*Richness*
Ịma ihe arụrụ	*Understanding the current trend*
Ịnọ mma	*Being good for somebody*
Ịnọ n'ofe	*Being in a better condition/state*
Ịsụ pụtụ pụtụ n'ofe	*successful person/ enjoying better life*
Iwete ọkụ	*A giver/being generous or active sexually*
Nkwọbi	*Sliced meat/fish mixed with vegetables*
Odeku	*Stout beer*
Ọkpa ọkụ	*Fine and smooth leg*
Pọọpọ nwa	*Pretty girl or lady with glowy skin*
Santana	*Pounded cassava*
Sherikoko	*Beautiful young lady/girl*
Tamtam	*Perfect/something that is very fine*
Yoriyori	*Something beautiful/sweet/good*

Characteristic word (okwu nke agwa): these are words that are used to describe a thing, a situation, condition of thing, behavior and lifestyle in a manner that only people that know what it means would understand. They may also be a descriptive expression of a specialty of a thing. It is not limited to natural things but include magical and diabolical slangs. Some of the jests/slang may come in the form of noun, phrase, clause, figure of speech, and so on. For example:

Igbo word	English translation
Adịgboroja	Fake or old-fashioned
Akpịrịko	A price gouger/ trickster
Akwunakwuna	Harlotry
Ashebi	Uniform dress by a group
Ata na-agba	Serious confusion
Ife ajụ	To charm and manipulate somebody
Ịgba tọọchị	Bribery/to give bribe
Ịja	Money
Ikechi mmadụ	To tie someone with evil power
Ịma mmadụ (IM)	Nepotism
Ịsa isi	Brainwashing
Nchọchọ	Money
Ndị eke	Police officers
Odeshi	protective charm
Okerieọnwụọ	poison/deadly substance or product
Ọkịrịka	Fairly used clothes/second hand clothes
Ọkụ enu/ọkụelu	Prostitute
Ọtapịapịa	Poisonous/deadly substance
Ọtụmọkpọ	undefendable and dependable charm
Tokumbo	Fairly used vehicles or wares

Mispronounced/Corrupt Words (Okwu Mkpọhie):
This is another way of word formation in Igbo language. Mispronounced Words/Corrupt Words (Okwu Mkpọhie) are usually foreign words that are pronounced incorrectly. Although, they may be categorized under borrowed/loan words, however, because many rightful Igbo words were set aside in an attempt to

stay according to the source that might fall under this new category.

Igbo self-westernization has a big role in this. Their effort to either anglicize or francization themselves (especially the young generation) is making some Igbo names for things disappear. Anglicization refers to the process by which a place or person becomes influenced by English culture or British culture, or a process of cultural and/or linguistic change in which something non-English becomes English. Likewise, Francization and other languages that are being copied in exchange for what Igbo names objects and things bear.

It is important to note that names of things that do not exist in Igbo lexeme but were borrowed qualify for Igbo dictionary standard words entries but corrupt words may not be considered especially when there is an Igbo name for the thing which foreign name has been acquired for.

The following are examples of Mispronounced Words/Corrupt Words (Okwu Mkpọhie):

Words	*Place of Origin*	*Source word*
Abada	English	*Haberdashery*
Afụ	English	*Half penny*
Aloo	English	*Hello*
Barangidi	English	*Blanket*
Bọkwụ	French	*Beacoup*
Brezi	English	*Brassier*
Dọbụrụbaa	English	*Double barrel*
Gadarum	English	*Guard room*

Ịchafụ	French	*Le chifon*
Karafish	English	*Crayfish*
Kọtụma	English	*Court (man) messenger*
Mbụrọda	English	*Umbrella*
Nkachiifu	English	*Handkerchief*
Ofesi	English	*Overseas*
Oloko	English	*Locomotive*
Oroma	Portuguese	*Orange*
Potoki	English	*Portuguese*
Sajiin	English	*Sergent*
Shimi	English	*Chemise (an under wear)*
Sọfịa	English	*Surveyor*
Tapoolu	English	*Tarpauline*

Loan Blend (Mbiọgwa)

Loan blend are words formed by joining and blending Igbo words with a foreign word often for descriptive purpose. This sometime may come from young people who have learned a foreign word for a thing that has Igbo name and who want to show that they know what both side calls an object or to specify what they mean if they cannot lay hold of any Igbo expression that would replace their foreign knowledge. For example:

Loan blend words	*Translation/meaning*
Efere *plastik*	Plastic plate
Ite *alụminọm*	Aluminum pot
Ite *pọọtụ*	Metal pot
Ngazị/ngaji *plastik*	Plastic spoon
Oche *plastik*	Plastic chair
Ọkụ *eletrik*	Electric light
Tekinụzụ	Technology

Ụzọ moto   Tarred road

In the above examples, the italicized words beside Igbo words are the loan foreign words that were blended with Igbo words. Many people have come to accept the usage of this blend, although in formal standard writing they are rarely used.

Informal words formed from jest/slnags, loan words or loan blend can have a negative impact on original Igbo words. It can facilitate the disappearing of lexeme that have existed for years. There are many Igbo words that were used in the past five decades that are today going down the road of extinction. For example:

	Igbo word	Translation
1.	ákpàtà/àlụbálá	measles
2.	Égbúgbú	tattoo
3.	éjù	earthenware
4.	ekpenta	leprosy
5.	ékú	wooden spoon
6.	ékwú	kitchen
7.	m kpílíté	a small wooden mortar
8.	mbụrụ	stick (that is aimed and thrown at a tree top)
9.	mkpà	scissors
10.	mkpú	room
11.	mkpúkè	woman's bedroom/house
12.	mpanaka	lantern
13.	ǹchìchè	yaw disease
14.	ńgigā	basket hanging (over kitchen's stove)
15.	óché ékwu	kitchen stool
16.	ògbòdù	the uninitiated (into the masquerade cult)
17.	ókpēsị	symbol of divinity
18.	ọkpọgā	a type of chair

19.	ọkù	clay bowl
20.	òkwú-álụsi	shrine
21.	ọtáńjélé	local eye pencil
22.	òtòlò	diarrhea
23.	ufie	a reddish powder for beautification
24.	ùgànị	famine
25.	ùkó	shelf/counter
26.	ùri	make up for women

Chapter 21

Synonyms and Antonyms
(Myiri Mkpụrụokwu na Okwu Mmegide)

Words in a language may semantically relate or differ from another, hence meaning relation. Meaning relation is considered using more than one word. When two or more words are considered in terms of their similarities and differences, meaning relation is employed to determine where they fall into. Synonym is a meaning relationship between two or more words that have different sounds and spellings but have similar or exact meaning.

Synonyms (Myìrì mkpụrụokwū):
A synonym is a word or morpheme (mkpụrụasụsụ) that means exactly or nearly the same as another word or morpheme (mkpụrụasụsụ) in the same language but often with different implications and associations. For example, in the English language, the words begin, start, commence, and initiate are synonymous.

Two or more words sharing the same semantic similarities are synonyms. Synonymous words are often times interchangeable in communicative effects. Although not in all context as we would see in the following description. The use of synonyms can help one avoid repetition and spice up expression.

Words have certain uniqueness that another that is supposedly alike may not have. As a result, certain Igbo synonyms word cannot always be used exactly the same way in a sentence. This gave rise to two forms of synonyms, namely:

- Absolute synonyms and
- Partial synonyms

Absolute Synonyms

Absolute synonyms are also known as exact, true, total, complete synonyms is a term used to describe two words have all meaning components in common and regarded as complete synonyms. When a word shares the majority of their meaning components with other words and share exactly the same communicative effect in every contexts in which they are used, such two words are classified as absolute synonymous.

Also, absolute synonymous words are interchangeable and can be used in similar environments all the time without a change in meaning. Some of the common English examples for absolute synonyms are: everybody/everyone, anybody/anyone, somebody/someone, frequently/often, rarely/seldom and so on. When all the contextual relations of two words are identical, they are considered as absolute synonymous words. For example:

Total synonyms	*Translation*
àchàrà/ọtọsí	*bamboo*
ákílū/ágbílū/ùgórò	*bitter kola*

ákụkụ/ágà	side
àkùpe/ǹkùfe/ǹkụcha	hand fan
ànyásị/ùchíchì/ùjíshì	night
ébírí/Ọgbọ	age-mate
éfè/óhérē	chance
égwú/úrí	song
érírí/ékwéré/ụdọ	rope
gírígírí/ńgálíngá	slim/thin
gùzó/kwụrụ	stand
ìbèríbè/ńzúzú	stupidity/silliness
kịrịkịrị/írighírí	tiny
kítàà/ùgbúà/ǹnwéé	now
ḿbá/òóló	no
mgbèdè/ùhúrúchì	evening
mkpà/ǹchà	scissors
náánī/sọọsọ	only
ǹkàtà/èkètè	basket
ǹkịtị/ụkpọrọ	nothingness
ọgụ/òtí	hoe
ògúgù/ípā	palm frond
ọmụ (nkwụ)/ọkpúkpà	newly sprout palm frond
ònwéghì/òméhè	nothing
ọsọọsọ/ńgwáńgwá	quickly/hurriedly
ótù/òfú/ńnáā	one
ụbàrá/mmánụ	many/plural/numerous
ùbé ḿgbā/ùbé òkpòkó	black pear
úbì/úgbō	farmland
ùwé/èfè/mweyì	cloth

Partial Synonyms

Partial synonyms also known as synonyms are words very similar to another but not identical in contextual application usage because of their incongruent meaning and inexactness in their associative meaning. These words often have the same communicative effect in some contexts but not in all contexts.

Also, partial synonyms can refer to words that are identical in meaning but fail to meet the condition of all-round application as in the case of absolute synonymy. These words have the same reference but are not encompassing in all aspects of associative meaning.

An example of partial synonyms in English language is vacant and empty. Whereas one can say, *vacant room* or *empty room*; it is incompatible to use them as in *vacant job* and *empty job*. Another example is *"work"* and *"job"*. One can say, *"I work in an office"* but cannot say *"I job in an office"*. The above two examples are partial synonyms in English language.

Partial synonyms	*Translation*
àzụ ụlọ/Òwèrè	*backyard*
búté/bútá/pátá	*carry/lift to*
ékwú ígwè/òshí ìtè/ákwụkwà	*tripod stove stand*
ghúò/síè	*cook*
kú/gbú (mmiri)	*fetch (water)*
kwá/dụ	*sew*
sú/sá (ákwà)	*wash cloth*
té/hịọ/fịá	*rub*

Partial synonyms result from three types of restrictions that exist in Igbo language. Contextual, collocational and connotative restrictions exist in Igbo words and are revealed when pairs of synonyms are placed in certain sentence or contexts of expression.

Therefore, there are basically three ways in which Igbo synonyms can be restricted in usage and they are as follows:

- Collocational restriction
- Connotative restriction and
- Contextual domain restriction

Before taking a look at each of the restrictions mentioned above, let us have a look at the overview of Standard Igbo synonyms based on common meanings as follows:

Synonyms	Meaning	Synonyms	Meaning
Ábàlị/Ùchíchì	Night	Ábụ̀/Ùkwé	Poem/Song
Àgbụ̀rụ̀/Ébó	Tribe	Ághá/Ọgù	War
Àmàmíhé/Àkọ	Wisdom	Átụ̀màtụ̀/Ámụ̀mà	Idea/Plan
Bé/Ụ̀lọ	House/home	Dúm/Nííḹē	All
Ényì/Ọyị	Friend	Èzí/Mbárá	Compound
Óyìbó/Bèkéè	English	Ńsọpụ̀rụ/Ùgwù	Respect
Ìbèríbè/Ńzúzù	Foolish	Ìgbé/Ákpàtị	Box
Íké/Úmé	Strength	Ìnyòm/Nwáànyị	Woman
Ísí-mkpē/Àjàdù	Widow	Òmùmé/Àgwà	Character
Ìzìzì/Mbụ	First	Jé/Gá	Go
Jédébé/Kwụsị	End	Mbídó/Mmàlíté	Beginning
Mkpọtụ/Ụ̀zụ̀	Noise	Mmēē/Ọbàrà	Blood
Mméhiè/Njọ	Sin	Mpàkó/Ńgàlá	Pride
Ngá/Mkpóóró	Prison	Ngáná/Úmé-ngwụ	Lazy
Ógè/Mgbè	When/Time	Ónyé ndū/Ónyé ísī	Leader
Ọchị/Ámụ	Laughter	Ọgbákọ/Ńzụ̀kọ	Meeting
Ọgbọ/Ébírí	Peer	Ọmikō/Èbérè	Mercy

Ọsọ ọsọ/Ṅgwá ṅgwá	*Quickly*	Sịrị/Kwùrù (Sị/kwú)	*Said*
Ùbì/Ụ́gbō	*Farm*	Ụ̀bịàm/Ógbènyè	*Poverty*
Ùgègbè/Ènyò	*Mirror*	Ụ̀ghá/Àsị	*Lie*
Ùhúrúchī/Mgbèdè	*Evening*	Úsà/Ázịzá	*Answer*
Ùwé/Ákwà	*Cloth/dress*	Ụjọ̄/Égwù	*Fear*
Ụ̀kwụ̀/Ọ̀kpà	*Leg*	Èbùmnúchè/Èbùmnóbì	*Intention*

1. Collocational restriction

Collocational restriction is a linguistic term that is used to refer to the fact that in certain two-word phrases or expressions, the meaning of an individual word is restricted to that particular phrase or expressions. Collocation is the tendency of words to co-occur with each other. It is a function of the relationship that words have together which make them stay together in certain expression. Words that are strongly attached together often restrict a member of a synonymous pair from co-occurring with lexical phrases. For example in English language, the adjective dry can only mean 'not sweet' in combination with the noun wine.

In Igbo language, the rule of specific selection of words operates within the innate linguistic knowledge of a speaker and allows him or her to match not only sounds and meanings in their message but place relational co-occurring words with each other. When selectional rule is observed in an expression, other synonymous member(s) will be collocationally restricted. Selectional restrictions are the semantic restrictions that a word imposes on an environment in which it occurs that restrict the use of another synonymous member.

The following are examples of collocational restriction in Igbo language.

Synonyms: Àmàmíhé/Àkọ
Meaning: Wisdom
1ˢᵗ instance: *Akọ* na uche   (permitted)
Translation: Wisdom
2ⁿᵈ instance: *Amamihe* na uche   (restricted)
Translation: Wisdom and mind

Synonyms: Dúm/niile
Meaning: All
1ˢᵗ instance: Ndị *niile* bịara ebe a ụnyaahụ (permitted)
Translation: Everyone that came here yesterday.
2ⁿᵈ instance: Ndị *dum* bịara ebe a ụnyaahụ (restricted)
Translation: Everyone(s) (pl) that came here yesterday.

Synonyms: Èbùmúchè/Èbùmóbì
Meaning: Intention
1ˢᵗ instance: *Èbùmúchè* edemede. (permitted)
Translation: Objective of study
2ⁿᵈ instance: *Èbùmóbì* edemede. (restricted)
Translation: intention of writing (different usage)

Synonyms: Èzí/Mbárá
Meaning: Compound (residential/home)
1ˢᵗ instance: *Ezi* na ụlọ/**Ezinụlọ** (permitted)
Translation: Family
2ⁿᵈ instance: *Mbara* na ụlọ (restricted)
Translation: Compund and house (different meaning)

Synonyms: Ìgbé/Ákpàtị
Meaning: Box
1ˢᵗ instance: *Igbe* mma (permitted)

Translation: Epitome of Beauty
2ⁿᵈ instance: *Akpatị* mma *(restricted)*
Translation: (Storage) box for beauty

Synonyms: Íké/Úmé
Meaning: Strength
1ˢᵗ instance: *Ike ọkpụkpụ (aka) (permitted)*
Translation: Physical strength
2ⁿᵈ instance: *Ume ọkpụkpụ (aka) (restricted)*
Translation: personal effort

Synonyms: Ìnyòm/Nwaáànyị
Meaning: Woman
1ˢᵗ instance 1: "**Ndị** *inyom* *(permitted)*
Translation: Women
2ⁿᵈ instance: Ụmụ *inyom* (restricted /lacks concordance)
3ʳᵈ instance: Ndị *nwaanyị* (restricted/lacks concordance)
4ᵗʰ instance: Ụmụ *nwaanyị (permitted))*
Translation: Women

Synonyms: Jé/Gá
Meaning: Go
1ˢᵗ instance: **Njé Njé/Njém** *(permitted)*
Translation: Travel/Journey
2ⁿᵈ instance: **Ngá ngá/Ngám** *(restricted)*
Translation: Ngángá as a compound word means "boasting."

Synonyms: Mbídó/Mmàlíté
Meaning: Beginning
1ˢᵗ instance: **Isi mbido** *(permitted)*
Translation: Beginning

2ⁿᵈ instance: Isi mmalite *(restricted)*
Translation: *head of beginning*

Synonyms: Mkpọtụ/Ụ̀zụ̀
Meaning: Noise
1ˢᵗ instance: Ụzụ akwa *(permitted)*
Translation: *Wailing*
2ⁿᵈ instance: *Mkpọtụ* akwa *(restricted)*
Translation: *Noise of cry*

Synonyms: Mméē/Òbàrà
Meaning: blood
1ˢᵗ instance: Ahụ na ọ*bara* Kraịst *(permitted)*
Translation: *flesh and blood of Christ*
2ⁿᵈ instance: Ahụ na *mmee* Kraịst *(restricted /no concordance)*

Synonyms: Ngá/Mkpọrọ
Meaning: Prison
1ˢᵗ instance: *Nga* mkpụrụ ọka *(permitted)*
Translation: *Life time imprisonment*
2ⁿᵈ instance: *Mkpọrọ* mkpụrụ ọka *(restricted /no concordance)*

Synonyms: Ńjédébé/Ńkwụsị/Mmechi
Meaning: End
1ˢᵗ instance: Isi *njedebe* *(permitted)*
Translation: *The end*
2ⁿᵈ instance: Isi *nkwụsị/mmechi* *(restricted /no concordance)*

Synonyms: Ónyé ndǔ/ Ónyé Ísī
Meaning: Leader

1st instance: *Onye isi oche (permitted)*
Translation: *Chairman*
2nd instance: *Onye ndu oche (restricted /no concordance)*

Synonyms: Ónyìbó/Bèkéè
Meaning: English/Foreign
1st instance: **Ala** *Bekee (permitted)*
Translation: *Foreign country*
2nd instance: *Ala Oyibo (restricted /no concordance)*

Synonyms: Ọchị/Ámụ
Meaning: Laughter
1st instance: **Ọchị** *eze (permitted)*
Translation: *Deceptive smile*
2nd instance: *Amụ eze (restricted /no concordance)*

Synonyms: Ọgụ/Ághá/Mgbá
Meaning: Fight/Struggle/War
1st instance: **Ọgụ** *na mgba (permitted)*
Translation: *Difficulty/up hilled*
2nd instance: *Agha na mgba (restricted /no concordance)*
Translation: *War and Fight*

Synonyms: Ùwé/Ákwà
Meaning: Cloth
1st instance: **Uwe** *mwụda (permitted)*
Translation: *Long loose gown*
2nd instance: *Akwa mwụda (restricted /no concordance)*
3rd instance: Obi/ukwu *akwa (permitted)*

Translation: Wrapper/Lappa/Pagne
4ᵗʰ instance: **Obi/ukwu *uwe*** *(restricted /no concordance)*

Synonyms: Ụjọ/Ég̀wù
Meaning: Fear
1ˢᵗ instance: **Onye *ụjọ* ọgwụ** *(permitted)*
Translation: A pharmacophobia/trypanophobia
2ⁿᵈ instance: **Onye *egwu* ọgwụ** *(restricted /no concordance)*

Synonyms: Ụkwụ/Ọkpà
Meaning: Leg
1ˢᵗ instance: **Ndị *ọkpa* atụrụ** *(permitted)*
Translation: Saboteurs
2ⁿᵈ instance: **Ndị *ụkwụ* atụrụ** *(restricted /no concordance)*

2. Connotative restriction

Connotation and Denotation are two principal methods of describing the meanings of words. Connotation refers to the wide array of positive and negative associations that most words naturally carry with them, whereas denotation is the precise, literal definition of a word that might be found in a dictionary.

Connotative meaning is an idea or quality that a word makes you think about besides its meaning. The *connotative meaning* of a word includes the feelings that people may connect with that word. A word may have negative/positive connotations for different people. For example, in English the word "fat" has negative connotations for many people because of its associative meaning to obesity. The word "childlike" has the connotation of innocence because of its associative meaning to children's innocence.

In Igbo language, the rule of specific selection of words in line with their connotative meaning operates within the innate linguistic knowledge of a speaker who would consider the intention of the message and make use of meaningful matching words that would not confuse the receiver.

The following are examples of connotative restriction in Igbo language would show you how a synonymous pair can produce different meaning in the same sentence or expression.

Synonyms: Ághá/Ọgù
Meaning: War/fight
1st instance: Eze na Emeka lụrụ ọgụ.
Translation: Obi and Obinna fought each other.
2nd instance: Eze na Emeka lụrụ agha.
Translation: Obi and Obinna fought the war.

Synonyms: Átụ̀màtụ̀/Ámụ̀mà
Meaning: Idea
1st instance: Anyị nwere amụma dị iche iche.
Translation: We have different programs.
2nd instance: Anyị nwere atụmatụ dị iche iche.
Translation: We have different ideas.

Synonyms: Ázịzá/ Ụsà
Meaning: Answer
1st instance: Kedụ ihe bụ azịza gị?
Translation: What is your answer?
2nd instance: Kedụ ihe bụ ụsa gị?
Translation: What is your response?

Synonyms: Mpàkó/Ńgàlá
Meaning: Pride
1st instance: **Onye ngala**
Translation: *A glamorous person.*
2nd instance: **Onye mpako**
Translation: *A prideful individual/ An arrogant person.*

Synonyms: Ńsọpụ̀rụ/Ùgwù
Meaning: Respect
1st instance: **Obinna enweghị nsọpụrụ.**
Translation: *Obinna has no respect.*
2nd instance: **Obinna enweghị ugwu.**
Translation: *Obinna has no good reputation.*

Synonyms: Ọmiíkō/Èbérè
Meaning: Mercy
1st instance: **Onye (obi) ebere**
Translation: *A merciful person.*
2nd instance: **Onye omiiko**
Translation: *A compassionate person.*

Synonyms: Úbì/Úgbó
Meaning: Farm
1st instance: **Ejere m n'ugbo m.**
Translation: *I went to my farm (land, fish pond, piggery, etc.).*
2nd instance: **Ejere m n'ubi m.**
Translation: *I went to my farmland.*

Synonyms: Ụkwụ̀/Ọkpà
Meaning: Leg

1st instance: **Ada nwere ụkwụ ogologo.**
Translation: Ada cuts corners.
2ns instance: Ada nwere ọkpa ogologo.
Translation: Ada has long legs (physical).

3. Contextual domain restriction

Synonyms, in Igbo language, are context sensitive as a result of the general idea or concept of usage combined with all other characteristics or particulars of the Igbo language lexemes. Contextually restricted synonyms are a condition in which a pair of lexemes is not able to substitute each other in all contexts. Context is a term used to describe words and sentence that surround any part of a written or spoken communication and that helps to determine its meaning. Words that are synonym lexemes are interchangeable with each other within contexts; they would be used as alternative in communication without any restriction.

A substitution test would reveal if a pair of synonyms are interchangeable in all contexts or not. When there is, at least, one context where a pair cannot be used interchangeably and give the same meaning, then one can draw a logical conclusion that they are not absolute synonyms. For example, ákwà/ùwé.

The general knowledge of an average Igbo native speaker views ákwà as to include any form of cloth material, and ùwé as being a specific term for "dress." And with other examples as shown below, one can understand that there are contexts where members of a synonymous pair are appropriate while in other contexts, they are not. When synonymous lexemes cannot substitute one another in all contexts based on the intuition of the native speaker, a speaker would conceptualize meanings within contexts and intuitively select the contextually appropriate member of a pair in a particular context of his or her message.

The result of this is that the uses of synonyms are based on how the Igbo native speakers conceive meanings in various contexts of written or spoken communication. When synonyms are used within the contexts of any communication, it is easier to determine the differences between them and to classify them as either absolute or partial synonyms. For example:

Synonyms: Ábàlị/Ùchíchì
Meaning: Night
1ˢᵗ instance: **Abalị dị egwu** *(compatible context)*
Translation: *Thief/Robber (idiomatic or metaphoric expression)*
2ⁿᵈ instance: **Uchichi dị egwu** *(incompatible context)*

Synonyms: Ábụ/Ùkwé
Meaning: Poem/Song
1ˢᵗ instance: **Ugonna na-abụ abụ.** *(Compatible context)*
Translation: *Ugonna is singing.*
2ⁿᵈ instance: **Ugonna na-abụ ukwe.** *(Incompatible context)*

The present continuous tense *"na-abụ"* does not go with ukwe. To get the same meaning one would have to use a present continuous tense *"na-ekwe"* to get the same meaning, e.g. *Ọ na-ekwe ukwe.* He/she is singing.

Synonyms: Ághá/Ọgụ
Meaning: War
1ˢᵗ instance: **Obi busoro m agha.** *(Compatible context)*
Translation: *Obi fought me.*

2nd instance: Obi busoro m ọgụ. *(Compatible context)*

Synonyms: Bé/Ụlọ
Meaning: House/home
1st instance: Ada nọ n'ụlọ. *(Compatible context)*
Translation: Ada is at home.
2nd instance: Ada nọ na be. *(Incompatible context)*

Synonyms: Dúm/Níilē
Meaning: All
1st instance: Ndị niile bịara ahịa ... *(Compatible context)*
Translation: All that came to the market ...
2nd instance: Ndị dum bịara ahịa ... *(Incompatible context)*

Synonyms: Ényì/Ọyị
Meaning: Friend
1st instance: Ada na nwata akwụkwọ kọleji na-ayị ọyị.
                (Compatible context)
Translation: Ada is befriending a college student.
2nd instance: Ada na nwata akwụkwọ kọleji na-ayị enyi.
                (Incompatible context)

Synonyms: Ìbèríbè/Ńzúzù
Meaning: Foolish
1st instance: Uchenna dara iberibe. *(Compatible context)*
Translation: Uchenna is foolish.
2nd instance: Ọ dara nzuzu. *(Incompatible context)*

Synonyms: Íké/Úmé
Meaning: Strength
1st instance: Ike ya gwụrụ m. *(Compatible context)*

Translation: I'm tired of him/her.
2ⁿᵈ instance: **Ume ya gwụrụ m.** *(Incompatible context)*
3ʳᵈ instance: **Ike dị n'okwu ahụ.** *(Compatible context)*
Translation: There is power in those words.
4ᵗʰ instance: **Ume dị n'okwu ahụ.** *(Incompatible context)*
5ᵗʰ instance: **Ọ bụghị site n'ike.** *(Compatible context)*
Translation: It's not by strength/might.
6ᵗʰ instance: **Ọ bụghị site n'ume.** *(Incompatible context)*

Synonyms: Ísí mkpē/Àjàdù
Meaning: Widow
1ˢᵗ instance: **Mgbeorie bụ ajadu.** *(Compatible context)*
Translation: Mgbeorie is a widow
2ⁿᵈ instance: **Mgbeorie bụ isi mkpe.** *(Incompatible context)*

Synonyms: Ìzìzì/Mbụ
Meaning: First
1ˢᵗ instance: **Na mbụ na mbụ̀...** *(Compatible context)*
Translation: First and foremost
2ⁿᵈ instance: **N'izizi n'izizi...** *(Incompatible context)*

Synonyms: Mkpọtụ/Ụ̀zụ̀
Meaning: Noise
1ˢᵗ instance: **Ụmụ akwụkwọ tụrụ ụzụ mgbe mgbịrịgba kụrụ.** *(Compatible context)*
Translation: students made noise when the bell rang.
2ⁿᵈ instance: **Ụmụ akwụkwọ tụrụ mkpọtụ mgbe mgbịrịgba kụrụ.** *(Incompatible context)*

Synonyms: Mméē/Ọbàrà
Meaning: Blood

1ˢᵗ instance: **Ọbara anaghị atụ asị.** *(Compatible context)*
Translation: Blood does not lie.
2ⁿᵈ instance: **Mmee anaghị atụ asị.** *(Incompatible context)*
3ʳᵈ instance: **Amaka na Emeka bụ otu ọbara.**
(Compatible context)
Translation: Amaka and Emeka are blood relations/ related by blood.

Synonyms: Mpàkó/Ńgàlá
Meaning: Pride
1ˢᵗ instance: **Tinye ngala n'egwu a.** *(Compatible context)*
Translation: Add glamour to the dance steps.
2ⁿᵈ instance: **Tinye mpako n'egwu a.** *(Incompatible context)*

Synonyms: Njọ/Mméhiè
Meaning: Sin
1ˢᵗ instance: **Ọ bụrụ na mmehie adịghị, mgbaghara agaghị adị.** *(Compatible context)*
Translation: To err is human and to forgive is divine
2ⁿᵈ instance: **Ọ bụrụ na njọ adịghị, mgbaghara agaghị adị.**
(Incompatible context)

Synonyms: Óge/Mgbè
Meaning: Time/When
1ˢᵗ instance: **Ada na-egbu oge.** *(Compatible context)*
Translation: Ada is wasting time.
2ⁿᵈ instance: **Ada na-egbu mgbe.** *(Incompatible context)*

Synonyms: Ọgbákọ/Ńzụkọ
Meaning: Meeting
1ˢᵗ instance: **Ezinụlọ Okeke ga-àkụ nzụkọ n'afọ ọzọ.**

	(Compatible context)
Translation:	Okeke family will host next year's meeting.
2ⁿᵈ instance:	**Ezinụlọ Okeke ga-àkụ ọgbakọ n'ọnwa ọzọ.**
	(Incompatible context)

Synonyms:	Sịrị/Kwùrù (Sị/kwú)
Meaning:	Said
1ˢᵗ instance:	**Ụkọchukwu sịrị anyị bịa.** *(Compatible context)*
Translation:	The priest/pastor said that we should come.
2ⁿᵈ instance:	**Ụkọchukwu kwuru anyị bịa.**
	(Incompatible context)

Synonyms:	Ụ̀bịàm/Ógbènyè
Meaning:	Poverty
1ˢᵗ instance:	**Ikenna bụ nwa ogbenye.** *(Compatible context)*
Translation:	Ikenna is poor.
2ⁿᵈ instance:	**Ikenna bụ nwa ụbịam.** *(Incompatible context)*

Synonyms:	Ùhúrúchī/Mgbèdè
Meaning:	Evening
1ˢᵗ instance:	**Ụwa mgbede ka mma.** *(Compatible context)*
Translation:	Life at old age is better.
2ⁿᵈ instance:	**Ụwa uhuruchi ka mma.** *(Incompatible context)*

Synonyms:	Ùwé/Ákwà
Meaning:	Cloth
1ˢᵗ instance:	**Kpuchie nwa ahụ akwa.** *(Compatible context)*
Translation:	cover that baby with a cloth.
2ⁿᵈ instance:	**Kpuchie nwa ahụ uwe.** *(Incompatible context)*
3ʳᵈ instance:	**Ndị otu ya kpuru/tụrụ ya akwa.**
	(Compatible context)

Translation: *Members of his group decorated/honoured him/her with a cloth (es)*
4th instance: **Ndị otu ya kpuru/tụrụ ya uwe.** *(Incompatible context)*
5th instance: **Nne Ugomma ma akwa n'obi.** *(Compatible context)*
Translation: *Ugomma's mom tied a wrapper over her chest.*
6th instance: **Ada ma uwe n'obi.** *(Incompatible context)*
7th instance: **Benye m akwa.** *(Compatible context)*
Translation: *Sell clothing (material) to me.*
8th instance: **Benye m uwe ọcha.** *(Incompatible context)*

Synonyms: Ụghá/Àsị
Meaning: Lie
1st instance: **Ọ tụrụ asị.** *(Compatible context)*
Translation: *He/she lied*
2nd instance: **Ọ tụrụ ụgha.** *(Incompatible context)*

Antonnyms (Okwu Mmegide)
An *antonym* is a semantic term for a word that has an opposite meaning to another word. It is a lexical term of relation that pivots on opposite in meaning of lexical items. Learning common Igbo antonyms sharpens your sense of Igbo language and expands your vocabulary.

Antonyms in the Igbo language can be grouped into:
1. Gradable
2. Complementary
3. Converse
4. Multiple taxonomies

Gradable antonyms: Graded (or gradable) antonyms are word pairs whose meanings are opposite and which lie on a continuous spectrum. In English language, they are typically pairs of adjectives that can be qualified by adverbs like very, quite, extremely, etc. So for example, we can say the tuition fees were expensive or were cheap.

However, as expensive and cheap are gradable antonyms, we can also qualify how expensive or cheap using adverbs like very, quite, extremely, etc.
Further examples of gradable antonyms are: bland/delicious, bright/dull, delicious/disgusting, friendly/unfriendly, hot/cold, interesting/boring, large/small, modern/old-fashioned, wet/dry and so on.

In Igbo language, similar to English, gradable can be tested with the addition of 'ezigbo' or 'tụ' or 'tụrụ' (which are measuring indicators) or by finding their intermediate words. The third line of each set is the application of the mid-interval words or scaling indicators, for instance:

Antonyms:	nnukwu/obere
Meaning:	big/small
1st instance:	Ofe Adanne kunyere m dịtụ obere.
Translation:	The soup that Adanne served me is quite small.
2nd instance:	Ofe Adanne kunyere m butụrụ ibu.
Translation:	The soup that Adanne served me is slightly big

Antonyms:	mma/njọ
Meaning:	beautiful/ugly

1ˢᵗ **instance:** **Adaeze mara** *ezigbo* **mma**
Translation: *Adaeze is very beautiful*
2ⁿᵈ **instance:** **Adaeze ma*tụrụ* mma**
Translation: *Adaeze is slightly beautiful*

Antonyms: ogologo/mkpụmkpụ
Meaning: tall/short
1ˢᵗ **instance:** **Emeka toro** *ezigbo* **ogologo**
Translation: *Emeka is very tall*
2ⁿᵈ **instance:** **Emeka to*tụrụ* ogologo**
Translation: *Emeka is slightly tall*

Antonyms: ọcha/oji
Meaning: fair/black
1ˢᵗ **instance:** **Nwamaka dị*tụ* ọcha/oji.**
Translation: *She is slightly fair/dark.*
2ⁿᵈ **instance:** **Nwamaka dị** *ezigbo* **ọcha/oji**
Translation: *She is very fair/dark*

Antonyms: nwata/okenye
Meaning: young/old
1ˢᵗ **instance:** **Okeke emeela** *ezigbo* **okenye.**
Translation: *Okeke is very old.*
2ⁿᵈ **instance:** **Okeke eme*tụ*la okenye.**
Translation: *Okeke is slightly old.*

Antonyms: warawara /obosara
Meaning: narrow/wide
1ˢᵗ **instance:** **Okporo ụzọ Aba dị** *ezigbo* **warawara**
Translation: *The road to Aba is very narrow*
2ⁿᵈ **instance:** **Okporo ụzọ Aba dị*tụ* warawara**

Translation: *The road to Aba is slightly narrow*

Antonyms: Ogbenye/ ọgaranya
Meaning: Poor-rich
1st instance: **Nwankwo nwere *ezigbo* ego**
Translation: *Nwankwo is very rich*
2nd instance: **Nwankwo nwe*tụrụ* ego**
Translation: *Nwankwo is slightly rich*

Antonyms: nso/anya
Meaning: near/far
1st instance: **Ụlọ akwụkwọ anyị dị *ezigbo* nso.**
Translation: *Our school location is very near.*
2nd instance: **Ụlọ akwụkwọ anyị dị*tụ* nso.**
Translation: *Our school location is slightly near.*

Antonyms: uju/ụkọ
Meaning: plenty/lack
1st instance: **Ọ nọ n'*ezigbo* uju ego.**
Translation: *He is in the season of (very) plenty of money.*
2nd instance: **Ọ nọ n'*ezigbo* ụkọ ego.**
Translation: *He is in the season of (extreme) lack of money.*

Antonyms: iwe/aṅụrị
meaning: angry/happy
1st instance: **Mmeri ahụ nyere ya *ezigbo* aṅụrị.**
Translation: *That victory made him/her very happy.*
2nd instance: **Mmeri ahụ we*tụrụ* ya iwe.**
Translation: *That victory made him/her very angry.*

Antonyms: ọsọọsọ/nwayọ-nwayọ

Meaning:	fast/slow
1st instance:	**Obinna na-eje*tụ* nwayọ-nwayọ karịa Uchenna.**
Translation:	*Obinna walks slightly slower than Uchenna.*
2nd instance:	**Obinna na-eje*tụ* ọsọọsọ karịa Uchenna.**
Translation:	*Obinna walks slightly faster than Uchenna.*

Antonyms:	ihụnaanya/akpọmasị
Meaning:	love/hate
1st instance:	**Ekene were *ezigbo* ihụnaanya n'ebe Adanna nọ.**
Translation:	*Ekene greatly love Adanna.*
2nd instance:	**Ekene were *ezigbo* akpọmasị n'ebe Adanna nọ.**
Translation:	*Ekene greatly hate Adanna.*

Antonyms:	ilo/enyi
Meaning:	enemy/friend
1st instance:	**Ngwere na Agwọ bụ *ezigbo* ndị ilo**
Translation:	*Lizard and Snake are arch enemies.*
2nd instance:	**Ngwere na Agwọ bụ *ezigbo* ndị enyi**
Translation:	*Lizard and Snake are very good friends.*

Antonyms:	ọkụ/oyi
Meaning:	hot/cold
1st instance:	**Mmiri ahụ dị*tụ* ọkụ (ṅara ṅara).**
Translation:	*The water is slightly hot (lukewarm).*
2nd instance:	**Mmiri ahụ dị*tụ* oyi (ṅara ṅara).**
Translation:	*The water is slightly cold (lukewarm).*

Antonyms:	isi/ ọdụ
Meaning:	head/tail
1st instance:	**Okwu ahụ enweghị isi nke o ji enwe ọdụ.**
Translation:	*Those words have neither head nor tail.*

2ⁿᵈ instance: **Okwu ahụ nwere *ezigbo* isi.**
Translation: *Those words are very important.*

Antonyms: mbido/njedewe
Meaning: beginning/end
1ˢᵗ instance: Ọ bịara na mbido emume ahụ.
Translation: He came at the beginning of the ceremony.
2ⁿᵈ instance: Ọ bịara na njedebe emume ahụ.
Translation: He came at the end of the ceremony.

All the examples above are scalable, that is, they have intermediate measurable values thus gradable.

Complementary antonyms: Complementary also known as non-gradable (or binary) antonyms are word pairs whose meanings are opposite and do not lie on a continuous spectrum (push, pull). In English language, complementary antonyms are pairs of words that are opposite in meaning, cannot be graded and are mutually exclusive. That means, they can exist independently of each other and there is no intermeadiate place inbetween. Examples of complementary opposites are: alive/dead, black/white, boy/girl, exit/entrance, lift/drop, push/pull, right/wrong, silence/noise, treat/punishment, yes/no, and so on.

In Igbo language, similar to English, complementary antonyms do not have any measuring indicators or intermediate words. They are absolute antonyms. The presence of one means automatic absence of the other. They are also complementary to each other, for instance:

Antonyms   **Meaning**

Ee/mba	yes/no
iheọma/iheọjọọ	right/wrong
ihiụra/ịmụanya	asleep/alive
nbuli/nbuda	lift/drop
nkịtịị/ụzụ	silence/noise
nwoke/nwaanyị	man/woman
ojii/ọcha	black/white
oke/nwunye	male/female
ọnwụ/ndụ	dead/alive
ọpụpụ/mbata	exit/entrance

Converse/Reverse antonyms: Converse (and reverse opposite) antonyms are word pairs where opposite makes sense only in the context of the relationship between the two meanings (teacher, pupil).

In English language, converse antonyms are pairs of opposites where one cannot exist without the other. For example to have a patient, you must be a doctor. Therefore, doctor and patient are complementary antonyms. Further examples of complementary antonyms are: above/below, defence/prosecution, doctor/patient, husband/wife, night/day, parent/child, plug/socket, policeman/criminal, teacher/student and so on.

In Igbo language, similar to English, converse antonyms describe a relation between two entities from alternate viewpoints. They are converse terms in the sense that when one is applied, the other automatically assumes the opposite side. It is also used to describe a relationship between antonyms in term of movement or direction, where one term describes movement in one direction, the other in the opposite direction. Examples of Igbo converse antonyms are as follows:

Antonyms:	Onyenkuzi/nwaakwụkwọ
Meaning:	Teacher/student
1ˢᵗ instance:	**Ọlụchi bụ Onyenkuzi anyị.**
Translation:	Ọlụchi is our teacher
	(Conversely, We're Ọlụchi's students)

Antonyms:	nne/nwa
Meaning:	mother/child
Instance:	**Mgbeorie bụ nne Onyeka.**
Translation:	Mgbeorie is Onyeka's mother.
	(Conversely, Onyeka is Mgbeorie's child)

Antonyms:	okwuu/ọnụụ
Meaning:	speaker/hearer
Instance:	**Akụchi bụ okwuu na mmemme anyị.**
Translation:	Akụchi is the speaker in our program.
	(Conversely, we're Akụchi's hearer/audience)

Antonyms:	ọgụegwu/ọgbaegwu
Meaning:	singer/dancer
Instance:	Ada bụ Ọgụegwu; anyị bụ ọgbaegwu.
Translation:	Ada is the singer and we are the dancer.

Antonyms:	di/nwunye
Meaning:	husband/wife
Instance:	**Emeka bụ di Ọlụchi**
Translation:	Emeka is Ọlụchi's husband.

(conversely Ọlụchi is Emeka's wife)

Antonyms:	Mgbago/mgbada
Meaning:	North/south
Instance:	**Kalụ is from the southern part of their country,**
Translation:	*Kalụ si n'akụkụ mgbada obodo ha.*

(conversely Kalụ is not from the north)

Antonyms:	akanri/akaekpe
Meaning:	Right-hand/left-hand
Instance:	**Emeka na-eme akaekpe.**
Translation:	*Emeka is left-handed.*

(conversely, Emeka is not right-handed)

Antonyms:	ọdịda anyanwu/ọwụwa anyanwu
Meaning:	west/east
Instance:	**Ndị Igbo si na ọwụwa anyanwu.**
Translation:	*The Igbo are from the east.*

(Conversely, The Igbo are not from the west)

Antonyms:	Bịa/gaa
Meaning:	Come/go
Instance:	**Eze ga-abịa ebe a.**
Translation:	*Eze will come here.*

(Inversely, Eze will not go there)

Antonyms:	Gaa/lọọ
Meaning:	Go/return
Instance:	**Ada ga-aga ahịa.**
Translation:	*Ada will go to the market.*

(Inversely. Ada has not return from the market)

Antonyms:	Ime/mpụta
Meaning:	In/out
Instance:	**Uche nọ n'ime ụlọ**
Translation:	Uche is in the house
	(Inversely, Uche is not out of the house)

Antonyms:	Gbago/gbada
Meaning:	Up/down
Instance:	**Obi si ya gbago elu ụlọ.**
Translation:	Obi told him/her to go up the stair of the house.
	(Inversely, Obi did not ask them to come down)

Antonyms:	nye/nara
Meaning:	Give/Receive (take)
Instance:	**Nye ya ego.**
Translation:	Give him/her money.
	(inversely, Do not recieve money from him/her)

Antonyms:	Ihu/azụ
Meaning:	Front/back
Instance:	**Gaa n'iru oche.**
Meaning:	Go to the front seat.
	(Inversely, don't go to the back seat)

Antonyms:	binye/biri
Meaning:	lend/borrow
Instance:	**Binye ya ego.**
Translation:	Lend him/her some money.
	(Inversely, do not borrow from him/her)

Multiple Taxonomies: Multiple taxonomies are groups or fields of words such as days of the week, months of the year, etc., that comprise a fixed system. As such, they are distinct from the pairs of opposites described above as they feature three of more items in the system. Further examples in English language include:
- fail/pass/merit/distinction,
- Mon-Tue-Wed-Thu-Fri-Sat-Sun,
- north/south/east/west,
- solid/liquid/gas,
- spades/hearts/diamonds/clubs,
- spring/summer/autumn/winter, and so on.

In Igbo language, multiple taxonomies refer to the classification of items that belong to one group. Market days are the most common taxonomy. It comprises: Eke, Orie, Afọ, Nkwọ. These four market days can only have an individual day each. That is, Eke market day can never be Orie, Afọ or Nkwọ on the same day. It means that the presence of one means the absence of others. Some groups of multiple taxonomies are closed systems that is no new member can be added to it. Igbo's market days is a typical example.

Birds: ọkụkụ (*fowl*), ọkwa, ọgazị (*guinea fowl*), ichoku (*parrot*), nza, obu, ikwikwii (*owl*), ọkịrị, torotoro (*turkey*) etc.

Colours: edoedo (*yellow*), akwụkwọndụ-akwụkwọndụ (*green*), ọbaraọbara/uhieuhie (*red*), urukpuurukpu (*blue*), ajaaja/ncharanchara (*brown*), oji (*black*), ọcha (*white*), awọawọ (*grey*), etc.

Vegetables: onugbu (*bitter-leaf*), ugu (*pumpkin*), nchaanwụ (*scent-leaf*), akwụkwọaṅara (*garden-egg leaf*), etc.

The three sets of antonyms above when one item in the group is active the rest are inactive. A woman who buys chicken/fowls did not buy guinea fowl or any other bird in the taxonomy. A shoe that is red in colour cannot be black at the same time. A soup that was prepared with scent-leaf, was not cooked with bitter-leaf unless if there were a mixture of vegetables in the soup.

ADVANCED IGBO LANGUAGE

Chapter 22

Parts of Speech
(Nkejiasụsụ Igbo)

There are eight categories that words are placed into based on what they mean and how they are used in a sentence.

Mkpoaha/ Aha (Noun)
A noun is a name of a person, place, thing or an idea.
Examples

English	*Igbo*
Classroom	Klaasị
Train	Ụgbọ oloko
Food	nri
Dog	Nkịta
Forest	Ọhịa
Table	Okpokoro
Joy	Ọṅụ

a. *Proper Noun (Ahaaka)*: A proper noun is the name given to something to make it more specific. It identifies a particular person, place, or thing (e.g., Nnamdi, Chidi, Awka, Ikwerre, Brian, California). Proper nouns differ from common nouns because common nouns are the words for something in general.

b. *Common Noun (Ahaizugbe)*: refers to people, places, or things in general e.g. abụ (song), ọṅụ (joy), okorobia (boy), nkịta(dog), obodo (city), ụbọchị (day). Common nouns are written with a capital letter only when they start a sentence.

c. *Collective Noun (Ahaigwe)*: refers to a set or group of people, places, animals, or things e.g. Ezinụlọ (family), akwụkwọ (books), igwe (multitude).

d. *Compound Noun (Ahaukwu)*: compound nouns are words for people, animals, places, things or ideas, made up of two or more words, e.g. umu-akwụkwọ (students), umuaka (children), ụlọ-akwụkwọ (school), ndi-ọrụ (workers), etc.

e. *Abstract Noun (Ahauche/Ahaechereche)*: this refers to ideas, qualities, conditions and things that do not exist physically e.g. ọṅụ (joy), enyi (friendship), ihunanya (love).

f. *Concrete Noun:* refers to people and things that exist physically e.g. mmadụ (person), ụwa (planet), osisi (tree), enwe (monkey).

g. *Countable Nouns (Aha-agutaraonu)*: countable nouns are nouns that can be counted individually; you can put a number before it as a quantity, e.g. Ụgbọ-ala abụọ (two cars), Nkịta anọ (four dogs), Ụmụnne atọ (three brothers), etc.

h. *Uncountable Nouns (Aha-Agutaonu)*: uncountable nouns refer to things that can't be individually counted, and don't take an indefinite article (a or an) in front of them e.g. ego (money), akụ (wealth), mmiri (water), egwu(music), ịhụnanya (love), etc.

Note that money is uncountable but ego-igwe (coin) or ego akwụkwọ (bank notes) are countable. Water is uncountable but glass of water is countable.

Nnochiaha (Pronoun)
Igbo pronouns, unlike other language, are not gendered as a result the same pronouns are used for male, female and inanimate beings. There are four singular pronouns (i, ị, o, and ọ) and two impersonal pronouns (a and e).

Every Igbo pronoun stands alone in a sentence. They do not join to verb or noun except they are in prefixed form, as in the case of first person singular and third person plural. The following are examples of standalone and prefixed forms of Igbo pronouns:

First person singular   *Igbo*
I went to market.   Ejere m ahia.
I asked a question.   Ajụrụ m ajụjụ.

2ⁿᵈ person singular   *Igbo*
You made my day.   Ị mere taa ụbọchịọma nye m.
You are kind.   Ị bụ ezigbo mmadụ.

3ʳᵈ person singular   *Igbo*
She is so beautiful   ọ maka/ ọ mara ezigbo mma

| He is handsome | ọ maka/ ọ mara ezigbo mma |
| It is so beautiful | ọ mara ezigbo mma |

3rd person plural	Igbo
They did the dishes	Asara efere.
They cooked food	Esiri nri

The following are various types of pronouns.

a. Subject Pronoun (Nnochiaha) is a word that takes place of a noun in a sentence. It functions as and acts as a substitute for a noun or nouns. Examples: I, you, it, they, we, he, she.

b. Personal Pronoun (Nnochionye): this type of pronoun refers to the speaker or the person spoken to, or to a person or things whose identity is clear, usually because they have already been mentioned. For example:

Subject

English	Igbo	Plural	Igbo
I/me	*m, mụ*	We	*anyị*
You	*ị, gị*	You	*unu*
He/she/it	*o*	They	*ha*
He/she/it	*ọ*	They	*ha*
He/she/it	*ya*	They	*ha*

Object

Me	*m/mụ*	Us	*anyi*
You	*gị*	You	*unu*
Him/her/it	*ya*	them	*ha*

c. *Impersonal pronoun (Nnochimpesin)*: Also known as impersonal pronoun, impersonal pronoun is used in a sentence to show non-specific beings, objects, or places. This can be used to represent countable noun or uncountable nouns; e.g. it (a, e). The two impersonal pronouns in Igbo language are a and e.

d. *Possessive Pronoun (Nnochinke)*: This type of pronoun is used in a sentence to show that something belongs to someone; e.g. my, our, your, his, her, its and theirs. There exists an independent form of each of the above possessive pronouns and they are: mine, ours, yours, his, hers, its, and theirs. For example:

English	*Igbo*
mine	nke m
Yours	nke gị
His	nke ya
Her	nke ya
Our/ours	nke anyị
Their/theirs	nke ha

e. *Demonstrative Pronoun (Nnochingosi)*: This type of pronoun is used in a sentence to point out specific things. There are only four demonstrative pronouns and they are: this, that, these and those. Examples in Igbo language are as follows:

English	*Igbo*
This	ihe a
That	ihe ahụ
These	ihe ndị a
Those	ihe dị ahụ

f. *Reflexive pronoun (Nnochionwe/Nnochinkowa)*: This type of pronoun is used in a sentence to refer to subject of the sentence. It is preceded by adverb, adjective, pronoun, or noun to which it refers, so long as that antecedent is located within the same clause. They end with the suffix 'self' (onwe); e.g. myself, yourself, himself, herself, oneself, itself, ourselves, yourselves, and themselves.

Examples:

English	Igbo
Myself	onwe/ Munwà
Yourself	onwe gi/ Ginwà
Himself	onwe ya
Herself	onwe ya
Oneself	onwe ya
Itself	onwe ya
Ourselves	onwe anyi/ Anyịnwà
Yourselves	onwe unu
Themselves	onwe ha

g. *Emphatic Pronoun (Nnochionweonye)*: This type of pronoun is used in a sentence to explain the action done by a noun without anyone's help. Examples of emphatic pronouns are the same form as reflexive pronouns. However, the difference between emphatic pronoun and reflexive pronoun is that reflexive pronoun acts as direct or indirect object in a sentence while emphatic pronouns are essentially unnecessary. For example:

I went to the hospital myself. (Reflexive pronoun)
E jere m ụlọ-ọgwụna nke onwe m.

The doctor himself treated me. (Emphatic pronoun)
Dọkịta na onwe ya lekọtara anya.

The word "myself" in the first sentence serves to reinforce that it was the subject (i.e. the president) that performed the action. Please note that emphatic pronoun can be removed from a sentence and the meaning of the sentence would still remain intact.

Verbs (Ngwaa)
a. *Infinitive Verbs (Isingwaa)*: This is a verb form that functions as a noun or is used with auxiliary verbs, and that names the action or state without specifying the subject. In Igbo language, the letter "ị" and "I" plus the root verb comprise the infinitive form of verb.

Examples:

English	Igbo root verb	English	Igbo root verb
to be	ịbu/ịdị	to bring	iweta
to buy	ịzụta	to call	ịkpọ
to chew	ịta	to come	ịbịa
to cook	isi nri	to cry	ibe akwa
to dance	ịgba egwu	to do	ime
to drink	ịṅu	to eat	iri (nri)
to enter	ịbanye/ịbata	to find/look	ịchọ/chọta
to follow	isoro	to forget	ichefu
to fry	ighe	to get	inweta
to give	inye	to go	ịga
to have/own	inwe	to hear	ịnụ
to hold	ijide	to know	ịma
to laugh	ịchi (chi a)	to learn	ịmụta
to leave	ịhapụ	to listen	ige nti
to look	ile (anya)	to mark	ịka (akara)

to get out	iputa	to play	igwu egwu
to pray	ikpe ekpere	to read	igu
to remember	icheta	to run	igba oso
to say	ikwu (okwu)	to see	ihu
to sell	ire (ahia)	to bathe	isa ahu
to sing	iguo abu/ ibuo abu	to sit	inodu
to sleep	irahu (ura)	to speak	isu
to stand	iguzo/ikuli	to stay	ino
to swallow	ilo	to take	iwere
to teach	ikuzi	to tell	igwa
to think	iche echiche	to throw	itu
to touch	imetu	to understand	ighota
to wait	ichere	to walk	iga ije
to wash	isa	to wear	iyi
to work	iru	to write	ide

b. *Linking Verbs (njiko ngwaa)*: This type of verb that connects a noun or a pronoun with a word that identifies or describes it; e.g. is, am, are, etc.
Examples:

English	Igbo
is	bu
am	bu
are	bu

c. *Auxiliary Verbs (Enyemaka ngwaa)*: This is a verb that changes or helps another verb, e.g. am, is, are, was, were, be, been, will, has, have, had, do, does, did. In Igbo language, auxiliary verbs often complement verb form to express an action in simple, continuous or future tense. When an auxiliary verb is complementing a simple participle, the auxiliary verb is joined to the complement with a hyphen. This is especially the case when the infinitive accompanying starts with a vowel. The hyphen is used to differentiate/separate the auxillary verb which is a form of prefix of the simple participle from main verb.

For example:
Igbo   *English*
1. Ben gà-enweta ụgbọ ala.   *Ben will catch the bus*
2. Eze nà-àbia ebe a.   *Eze is coming here*
3. Ngọzị ga-àbịa   *Ngọzị will come*
4. Ọ ga-àbịa   *He/She will come*
5. Eze na-abịa   *Eze is coming*
6. Ọ na-abịa   *He/She is coming*

However, when the auxiliary verb takes on the suffix of negation, it is written separately from the complement without a hyphen and as a one word with the suffix.
For example:
Igbo   *English*
1. Ngọzị agaghị àbịa   *Ngọzị will not come*
2. Ọ gaghị àbịa   *He/She will not come*
3. Eze anaghị abịa   *Eze is not coming*
4. Ọ naghị abịa   *He/She is not coming*

Conjunction (Njikọ)
Conjunction: A conjunction is a word that joins words or groups of words in a sentence together, e.g. and, but, yet, because, so,

Igbo	English
kama	instead of
mgbe ahụ	then
rue	until
tupu	before
maka	as, so
otu	as, that
mana/kama	but, if, that, whether
na	and, that
ka mgbe	since
ka	so that, that
n'ihi	because
ma ọ bụ	or
ọzọkwa	moreover

Examples:

Igbo	English
a. Achọrọ m Ji kama Garri	I want Yam instead of Garri
b. Eri kwala nri, tupu m gawa.	Do not eat until I go
c. Maka na ọ dịmma, ka m jịrị rie ya	As this is good, I enjoyed it
d. Ọ dị mma otu osi buru izu ụka.	It is good, as it is weekend
e. Ihe a mara mma mana ọdị oke ọnụ	This is good, but expensive
f. Mụ na gị na-eje ahịa	You and I are going to shop

Adjective (Nkowaha)

An adjective is a word that describes or gives more information about a noun or pronoun. It tells you what kind, how many, or which one. The following are examples of adjectives:

Igbo	English	Igbo	English

ala	*low*	ọsịsọ	*fast*
chakoo	*empty*	elu	*high*
iwe	*angry*	ihere	*shy*
nsọ	*holy/sacred*	anya	*far*
obi ụtọ/añụrị	*happy*	obi ọjọọ	*sad*
ọcha	*bright*	ọcha	*clean*
ocha	*light*	oji	*dark*
ogologo	*long*	ntakịrị	*short*
ohu/ohuru	*new*	ochie	*old*
ọjọọ	*ugly*	ọjọọ	*bad*
ọkụ	*hot*	oyi	*cold*
ọma/mma	*beautiful*	ọma	*good*
siri ike	*hard*	dara ọnụ	*expensive*
ukwu	*big*	nta	*small*
ụtọ	*sweet*	ilu	*bitter*

Demonstrative adjectives are used to modify a noun so that we know which specific person, place, or thing is mentioned. Examples of demonstrative adjectives in Igbo language are: ahụ (that). Nke a (this), ndị ahụ (those), ndị a (these). In Igbo language, demonstrative adjectives follow the noun they are modifying.

For example:
Igbo	English
Nye m kalama ahụ	*Give me that bottle.*
Achọrọ m akwụkwọ ndị ahụ	*I want those books.*
Ọ chọrọ izute ya ụbọchị ahụ	*He wanted to meet her that day.*
Mango ndị a na-ere ure	*These mangoes are rotting.*
Apụghị ichefu ihe ahụ mere	*I can't forget that incident.*
Ụmụ ntakịrị ndị ahụ were iwe	*Those children were angry.*

Mkpịsị odide ahụ bụ nke m   *This pen belongs to me.*
Ụlọ ahụ nwere ụlọ-ahịa   *That building has a shop.*

Adverb (Nkwuwa)
An adverb is a word that describes a verb, adjective, or another adverb by giving more information about how or when something happens. It tells how, when, where, or to what extent, e.g. loudly, slowly, quickly, finally, always, tomorrow.

Igbo	English
a. Ọ na-agụ egwu n'olu dara ụda	She sings loudly.
b. Ọ gbara ọsọ ngwa ngwa	He/she ran quickly.
c. Ọ kwuru okwu n'olu dị jụụ	He/she spoke softly.
d. Eze kwara ụkwara n'olu dara ụda	Eze coughed loudly.
e. Ọ na-afụ Ọja nke oma.	He plays the flute beautifully.
f. Ha riri achịcha bekee n'anyaukwu	They ate the cake greedily.

Interrogative adverbs are used to ask a question. In Igbo, a question can only be initiated by either an interrogative or a personal pronoun. Following interrogatives are commonly used:

Igbo	English
Kedụ	*how, when, where, which?*
ebee	*where, which place?*
olee	*how much, how many?*
onye	*Who?*
gịnị/ọ gịnị?	*What?*
kedụ?	*How?*
maka gịnị?	*Why?*
ma ncha	*Never*
tara akpụ	*Rarely*

mgbe ụfọdụ	*Sometimes*
mgbe niīle	*Usually*
mgbe niīle	*Always*
nkeọma	*Very*

Preposition (Mbuuzo)

Preposition: A preposition is a word that describes a relationship between a noun or pronoun and another word in a sentence, e.g. at, on, in, across, besides, during, for, of, to, with, throughout etc. It goes before a noun or pronoun to specify a place, position or time. In Igbo, there is only one preposition "na". When preceding a vowel, it drops its vowel sound and letter and takes on the tone of noun that follows it. It is written as n'.

Examples:

Igbo	*English*	*Igbo*	*English*
na	*and*	n'okpuru	*under*
tupu	*before*	n'ikpeazụ	*after*
n'ime	*inside*	n'ihe/n'ilo	*outside*
na	*with*	mana	*but*
maka	*for*	si	*from*
je	*to*	ime	*in*

Examples:
ọ dï n'elu akwa ndina.	*it is on top of the bed.*
ọ dï n'okpuru akwa ndina.	*it is under the bed.*
ọ dï n'ime akpati	*it is inside the box.*
ọ dï n' akụkụ akwa ndina.	*it is beside the bed.*
ọ nọ n'ụlọ.	*he/she n is in the house.*
ọ dï n'elu aja.	*it is on sand.*

In combination with a noun, it can specify the location of the preposition in more detail:

Noun	Mkpoaha	Preposition	Mbuuzo
top	elu	in, at, on	na (common)
top	elu	up	n'enu
underside	okpuru	under, below	n'okpuru
interior	ime	inside	n'ime
edge	ọnụnụ	on top of	n'onunu
beside	n'akụkụ		

Interjection (Ntimkpu)

An interjection is a word or phrase that expresses a strong feeling or an emotion, e.g. Hurrah, Yippee! Wow! Oh, no! Ouch, Oops, Aha, Eww, etc. Interjections are divided into six types namely; greeting, joy, surprise, approval, attention and sorrow.

a. Interjections for Greeting (Ntimkpu nke ekele): This type of interjection is used in a sentence to indicate the emotion of warmth to a person or group of people during meeting with them. Examples:

English	Igbo
Hello!	Ndeewo!
Hello Igbo people	Igbo Kweenu! Yee

b. Interjections for joy (Ntimkpu nke ọnụ): This type of interjection is used in a sentence to indicate immediate joy and happiness when a happy occasion occurs.

Examples:
Wow!   Ewo!

Good!	Ezigbo!
Hurrah!	Iji ya!

c. *Interjections for Attention (Ntimkpu nke akpọmoku):* This type of interjection is used in a sentence to draw attention of someone to something.

Examples:
English	Igbo
Look!	Lee anya!
Behold!	Lee!
Listen!	Ge Ntị!
Shh!	Shh!

d. *Interjections for approval (Ntimkpu nke nnabata):* This type of interjection is used in a sentence to express a strong sense of approval or agreement for something that has happened or something that someone did.

Examples:
English	Igbo
Well done!	Daalụ!
Brilliant	Akonuche!
Bravo!	Agụ/Dike!
Wait!	Chelu!
Sure!	Isee!

e. *Interjections for surprise (Ntimkpu nke mberede):* This type of interjection is used in a sentence to express a strong sense of surprise about something that happened or something that someone did.

Examples:

English	Igbo
What!	Gini!
Oh!	Ewo!
Ah!	Ah Ah!

f. Interjections for sorrow Ntimkpu nke iriuju): This type of interjection is used in a sentence to express the emotion of sadness or disappointment about something that happened.

Examples:

Alas!	Ewo!
Oops!	Ha yie!
Ouch!	Ha yie!
Ah!	Ah ah!

Index

A

Abịdịị 28, 29
Acoustic phonetics 109
Acronyms 179, 222, 232
Active articulator 138, 139
Adjective .... 286; Demonstrative
Adverb .... 288; Interrogative Adverbs
.... 288
Affixes 177, 179, 180, 187
Agglutination 180
allomorph 197, 206
Alphabet: Igbo Alphabet 51
Alveolar ridge 141, 142, 156
Antonnyms 264
Articulatory Phonetics 109
Auditory phonetics 110

B

Bilabial 121, 133, 159
Blending 179, 222, 232
Bound Morphemes 176

C

Chroneme 115
Class-Changing 189
Class-Maintaining 188
Clipping 179, 222, 223
Coined Words 225
Compounding ..125, 179, 222, 224, 225
Conjunction 285
Consonant: Elision 65
Consonants ..12, 19, 37, 44, 45, 46, 52, 56, 64, 65, 66, 68, 71, 72, 74, 75, 107, 108, 110, 112, 118, 120, 121, 122, 131, 134, 137, 146, 147, 151, 156, 158, 161, 163, 172
Consonants: letters 64
Contour tone 120
Corrupt Words 240, 241

D

Derivational morphemes 187
diacritical marks 13, 41, 67
Diacritics 66
Diagraphs 11, 46, 65
Diphthong 55

E

Enclitic 181, 194
Epiglottis 142, 157
Esophagus 142, 157
Etymology 212
Extentional suffix 187, 191

F

Free morpheme 175
Functional morphemes 176

G

Gerund 181, 182, 197, 201
Glottalic airstream 130
Grapheme. 19, 111, 112, 137, 138, 143, 147

H

Hard palate 141, 142, 157
Heavy Vowel 45, 53
Homograph 85
Homonyms 82, 83
Homophones 82, 83, 84

I

Infinitives 181, 182, 197, 199, 200, 201
Infixes 180, 184, 185
Inflectional suffixes 192
Interjection .... 290; Approval
.... 291; Attention
.... 291; Greeting
.... 290; joy
.... 290; surprise
.... 291
Intonation 119
Isuama Igbo Studies 29

J

Jests 234, 235, 236, 237, 238, 239

L

labiodental 134
Larynx 142, 157
Lexeme 214
Lexical morphemes 176
Lexicology 1, 209, 211, 212, 213
Light Vowel 45, 53
Linguistic Ambiguity 79
Loan Blend 242
Loan Word 227
lungs 110, 129, 130, 134, 138, 146

M

Mazi Ọnwụ committee 43
Minimal pairs 112
Mispronounced Words 240, 241
Monophthong 54, 56
Morpheme 167, 168, 171, 172, 175
Morphology 1, 165, 167, 179
Multiple Taxonomies 274

N

Nasal cavity 141, 142, 156
Noun .... 277; *Abstract Noun*
.... 278; *Collective Noun*
.... 278; *Common Noun*
.... 278; *Compound Noun*
.... 278; *Concrete Noun*
.... 278; *Countable Noun*
.... 278; *Proper Noun*
.... 278; *Uncountable Noun*
.... 279
Noun agent 181, 183, 197, 202, 203
Noun instrument .. 181, 183, 198, 203, 204
Nsibidi 25, 26, 27, 28, 29
nterjection: sorrow 292

O

Onomasiology 213
organ of speech 129
Orthography ... 1, 15, 17, 22, 25, 37, 38, 41, 43, 215

P

Participles 181, 197, 198
Past tense 198, 204, 205

294

Pharynx 142, 157
Phoneme 111, 113, 114, 117, 118, 122, 137, 148, 168
Phonemes.107, 108, 117, 118, 131, 151
Phonemic Analysis 111
Phonetic transcription 151
Phonetics 105, 107, 108, 109, 110, 151, 155
Phonology 1, 105, 107
*place of articulation*110, 134, 138, 140, 147
Place of Articulation 137, 140
Plural 198, 205, 206, 280
Prefixes 180, 181
Preposition................................... 289
Pronoun . 279; *Demonstrative Pronoun* .... 281; *Emphatic Pronoun* .... 282; *Impersonal Pronoun* .... 281; Personal Pronoun .... 280; *Possessive Pronoun* .... 281; Subject Pronoun 280
prosody 118
Prosody... 107
Pulmonic airstream 129
punctuation: apostrophe...... 101; colon .... 101; comma .... 100; ellipsis ....104; exclamation .... 103; full stop .... 99; hyphen .... 101; parentheses .... 102; question marks ....100; quotaation marks ....102; semi-colon .... 100; slash 103
Punctuation.. 99

R

Reduplication 179, 222, 230, 231

S

Segmental phoneme....................... 118
Semasiology 213
Slang... 234
soft palate 131, 132, 141, 157, 162
Spelling rules 71
Stress.................................... 119, 216
Suffixes................................. 180, 186
Supra-segmental phonemes 118
Synonyms...... 245, 246, 247, 249, 251, 252, 253, 254, 255, 256, 257, 258, 259, 260, 261, 262, 263, 264

T

The SPILC.. 39
The Union Igbo Studies 34
Tonal: Accent Marks 66
Tonal Marking 13, 115
Toneme... 114
Tongue 132, 133, 142, 157
Trachea.................................. 142, 157
transcription 143, 144, 151, 152

U

Uvula 142, 157
uvular.. 134

V

Velaric airstream............................ 130
Velum..................................... 141, 157

Verb .... 283; *Auxillary Verbs* .... 284; *Infinitve Verbs* .... 283; *Linking Verbs* 284
Vocal cord 142, 157
vowel: Regressive Assimilation 59
Vowel: **Assimilation**. 56, 57, 58; Elision .... 56, 63; Heavy Vowel .... 53; Light Vowel .... 53; Progressive Assimilation .... 57; Vowel Harmony 53

Vowel harmony 53, 74, 125
Vowels..11, 44, 52, 123, 144, 145, 146; letters............. 52; Nasalized Vowels 66

W

wait 284
wash 284
Word Formation 221
work 102, 284

Other book by the Author:

1. Comprehensive Igbo Langauge
2. Syntax and Semantics in Igbo language
3. Writing and Literary Devices in Igbo Language.
4. Wild Animals Coloring book in Igbo Language
5. Farm Animals Coloring book in Igbo Language
6. Water Animals Coloring book in Igbo Language
7. Birds Coloring book in Igbo Language
8. Insects Coloring book in Igbo Language

ADVANCED IGBO LANGUAGE

ADVANCED IGBO LANGUAGE

ADVANCED IGBO LANGUAGE